inside
pocket billiards

championships and tournaments won by steve mizerak

United States Open Championship—1970, 1971, 1972, 1973
United States Masters Championship—1969, 1970, 1972
Stardust Open—1969
Michigan Open—1971
Eastern States Classic—1972
New Jersey State Championship—1967, 1968, 1969
United States Masters Nine-Ball Championship—1971.

SECOND PLACE
TV Tournament of Champions—1966
Los Angeles World Championship—1970

THIRD PLACE

International Pocket Billiard Championship—1968
United States Open Championship—1969

HIGH RUN
In Tournament Competition

150 (150-point-total match)
125 (125-point game)

In Exhibition

289

inside pocket billiards

steve mizerak

with
joel h. cohen

HENRY REGNERY COMPANY•CHICAGO

Library of Congress Cataloging in Publication Data

Mizerak, Steve, 1944-
  Inside pocket billiards.

  1. Billiards. I. Cohen, Joel H., joint author. II. Title.
GV891.M69   794.7's   73-6478

Published by Henry Regnery Company, 114 West Illinois Street,
    Chicago, Illinois 60610

Manufactured in the United States of America

Library of Congress Catalog Card Number: 73-6478

International Standard Book Number: 0-8092-8908-3 (cloth)

                                        0-8092-8907-5 (paper)

preface

When I was a college student, I was ineligible to participate in ACU-1 collegiate billiards because I had already attained professional status. But I did win second place in a National Collegiate Essay Contest with the following essay about my early billiards career.

Those Smoke-Filled Rooms

I was four years old when for the first time in my life I was brought into the town pool hall. As I entered the room I could see barely ten feet in front of me. The smoke was so thick that my lungs could hardly stand the odor of the cigars and cigarettes that almost everyone in the room was smoking. The owner of the pool hall was quite disturbed when I was set free of my father's hand to roam around and watch what was happening around the room. The men were all talking and some were playing pool. I didn't know whether to stand or sit.

Just as I was sitting down on a rather large bench, my father finished talking with some friends and we started to leave. As we were going out the door, one of the men thought it would be funny to place me on a pool table and hand me a cue stick to see what would happen. The owner didn't want me on a pool table for fear that I might break something, but after some talking, he relented. Then my father picked me up and put me on one of the pool tables.

The men in the room had put two balls on the table and handed me a cue stick that was twice as big as I was at the time. Then suddenly I put my hands on the table in a professional manner and easily stroked the 8-ball into the side pocket. The men's laughter changed to silence. No one knew what to say or do. My father was stunned. Then in amazement he picked me up from the table and we started to walk towards the exit. As my father started to open the door, the owner came running up to us and, with a big smile, invited my father to bring me back any time he wanted. During the next two years, I entered the pool hall frequently, practicing and learning all there is to know about the game that a six-year-old could learn.

At eight years of age, I started playing with some of the older men in the pool hall. My skill had progressed to the point where I could beat some of the men I played. Some of the men got very frustrated when an 8-year-old child beat a man of 40 or 45 in a game especially made for men. I was what one might call a gifted individual. At 12 my skill had grown profoundly and I had gained much attention throughout the state. People couldn't believe a 12-year-old boy could play pool as well as a 40-year-old man.

When I was 13 I started giving exhibitions throughout the New York and New Jersey area. My first exhibition was in the biggest city in the world, New York. The pool hall at which I was to play was located right in the heart of the city. As we were walking to my first exhibition we passed Times Square and many large buildings. As we stopped for a red light I looked around and saw all types of people hustling and bustling about. There were people with beards as long as three feet and mustaches as big as handlebars on a bicycle. As we started walking again I was amazed by the theatres and nightclubs all along the most famous street in the world, Broadway.

When we reached the entrance to the pool hall I looked around to see what a 13-year-old boy doesn't normally see. Right across the street from where we were standing was New York's most famous nightclub, the Latin Quarter. As I watched I saw many people get out of their cars and step on the red carpet that was rolled out for special guests. The guests were dressed in mink coats and tuxedos, and just for a moment I placed myself in one of the tuxedos and imagined I was escorting my school sweetheart. Then my father pulled my arm and we started walking up the stairs to the pool hall. When we opened the door I saw many strange faces and they were all waiting for me to start my exhibition. But I did see some familiar faces that I had seen previously in books and magazines. There were such stars as Luther Lassiter, who ate so many hamburgers they called him "Wimpy," and Jimmy "Cowboy" Moore, who was wearing his ten-gallon hat and leather riding boots. My opponent was the third best player in the city of New York. I was very nervous, so nervous that my hands were shaking and I could hardly talk. Many strange eyes were on me and I felt very uncomfortable. The exhibition that I was in consisted of a match of straight pool and ten fancy trick shots. The straight pool game started with my breaking the rack and trying to play it safe by not giving my opponent an easy shot. I made a perfect break, and when my opponent missed his first shot I felt very relieved that I would get first opportunity to get in the scoring column. I ran a string of 37 and missed a very simple shot in the side pocket. The game progressed very rapidly. Before I realized what was happening, my opponent overtook my score and shot out into the lead. Our game was to 100 points. The score was 94 to 78 in favor of my opponent, and he was up at the table. I figured the game was lost, but my opponent was overconfident and he missed an easy bank shot.

Now it was my turn. I ran a string of 22 points and won the game. The ovation the crowd gave me was tremendous, so loud that the applause could be heard three blocks away. When the noise quieted, I proceeded to show several trick and fancy shots. My repertoire included many shots that were very deceiving to the audience. My exhibition ended in spectacular fashion by my sinking six balls in one shot. I left the pool hall that night a very proud individual. The next day my name was mentioned in many newspapers and magazines throughout the metropolitan area. I was the talk of the billiard world.

The years between 13 and 19 were very profitable and successful. I played many exhibitions during this time and also won the New Jersey State Championship at the age of 18. When I was 19, I received my first break to gain national recognition. I was contacted by a large television studio about to film a tournament for national television. I played in this tournament and finished a close second. At the end I received a $4,000 check. The next few years found me gaining worldwide recognition as one of the greatest pool players in the world.

At present I rank among the top ten pool players in the world. To date I have never finished lower than eighth in any worldwide competition. I have finished second, fourth, fifth, seventh and eighth in these five championships. Soon, I hope, I will become world champion, a dream that I have had since I put the 8-ball in the side pocket when I was four years old.

The town pool hall where I made my debut as a child prodigy was a dark, dingy place compared to the bright, clean billiard parlors of today. Instead of being places no respectable lady would enter, billiard parlors are now set up to provide the whole family with safe, pleasant recreation. One thing remains the same, though—pool is still one of the best ways for people to relax, forget their worries, and have a good time.

In this book we'll be concentrating on pocket billiards, also known as *pocket pool* or *straight pool*. Pool has some advantages over other sports. There is no problem with the weather. You need only a small area in which to play. You don't need to be particularly strong or tall in order to play well. And, because size and strength are relatively unimportant factors, the game equalizes generations and sexes. I was beating grown men when I was only 12. Mine was an exceptional case, but there's no reason you can't at least hold your own with older players or better physical specimens. Billiards isn't expensive. There's no body contact, so you don't have to worry about getting your glasses or your bones broken. It can help you develop keen eyesight and good coordination.

The fact that you're planning to read this book means you don't have to be convinced that pocket billiards is a great game.

If you're starting out, you'll want to pay close attention to the fundamentals. If you've been playing for a while, there are tips here that will help you improve. Everyone—even a champion—can get better.

No matter what your playing level is, your main improvement will come from the experience of playing. The book, therefore, is just a foundation—a good one, I hope. Remember, the main object of the game is enjoyment. The better you play pool, the more you'll enjoy it. So let's master the fundamentals—and rack 'em up.

Steve Mizerak

contents

TAKE A FEW PRACTICE SHOTS . . . before you begin a game
on an unfamiliar table, or before you buy or use a cue stick.

chapter 1
BEFORE YOU BEGIN

First, let's look at the equipment you will use in pocket billiards.

THE TABLE

The standard pocket billiards table is 4½ by 9 feet, the size you'll find in most billiard parlors. In your home, you will most likely have a smaller table, since few houses have the large playing area that you need for a standard table. Tables come in all sizes: the smallest is 3 by 6 feet.

In the 1930s and 1940s, pocket billiards was played on a 5- by 10-foot table. You might not think that 6 inches in width and 12 inches in length would make that much difference, but, believe me, it does. The extra distance made it much more difficult to make shots. The 5- by 10-foot tables are now made only to special order.

With pool tables, as with just about anything else in life, you get what you pay for. You can get full-sized tables for

$100—these usually have honeycomb or plywood playing surfaces. But really good tables range in price from about $500 to $1,500, and generally have slate beds. A slate table may run as high as $2,500 for a fancy, custom-made job with leather on the side, but it is the best buy because it doesn't warp.

The slate used in a good table is very heavy—½ to 1 inch thick—and rests on a wood support. (Don't try to move a slate table, because you're liable to hurt your back and crack the slate or the floor on which the table is standing.)

The playing area of the table is known as the *bed* (Diagram 1). It consists of the cloth-covered slate, the *rails* along the inner edge, off which the balls carom, and the *pockets*. One end of the table, the one from which the *cue ball* is hit to start a game, is called the *head*. The opposite end is known as the *foot*. About a third of the way from the head of the table, midway between the sides, is a cir-

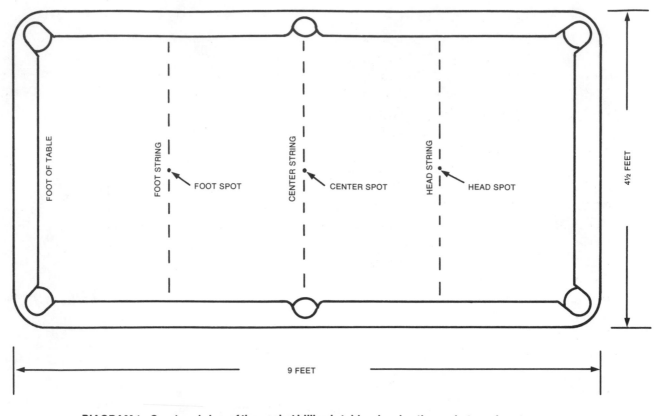

FOOT OF TABLE

FOOT STRING

FOOT SPOT

CENTER STRING

CENTER SPOT

HEAD STRING

HEAD SPOT

4½ FEET

9 FEET

DIAGRAM 1. Overhead view of the pocket billiards table, showing the pockets and spots.

cle known as the *headspot*. An imaginary line through this spot from one side of the table to the other is called the *head string*. Similarly, about a third of the table length from the foot is a circle known as the *foot spot*, and an imaginary line through it is called the *foot string*. In the center of the table is the *center spot*. The imaginary line through the center spot is called—as you may have guessed—the *center string*.

The cloth used for the bed of a pool table varies in type and color. The most common color is green, but owners of pool parlors have started to beautify their establishments, and now you might find any color. Actually, gold is the color that is probably easiest on the eyes. It's not advisable, however, to play on a color

that you'll play on only occasionally. It will hurt your game. So try to play on the same color all the time. Since green is still the most common color, you're probably better off playing on green tables, if you can.

When the cloth begins to wear out, the speed of the balls may be affected. If you own a table, be prepared to re-cover it every year or so, depending on how much use you give it.

If proper care is taken, the rails or cushions do not have to be changed as often as the cloth, because the balls don't roll directly over the cloth on the cushions.

A pocket billiards table has six pockets—one in each of the four corners and one halfway along each side. The size of the pockets may vary considerably. Some players feel that today's pockets are too large and they long for the days when pockets were smaller and shots had to be more precise. But modern tables don't give anything away.

The Table's "Personality"

Every table has its own "personality," and a championship player will shoot one or two frames to test it out. He or she will shoot a few balls down the rail and knock a few into the side pockets hard to determine how tough the pockets are. Especially if the cloth is worn, an older table may have a *drift* to one side or another, and a player wants to know this before the game begins. In championship play, contestants are usually given new tables on which to compete. Even then, they check out the tables to become familiar with their "feel." It's a good idea for you to do the same before you start a game.

Tables for Other Games

In this book, we'll be talking about many different games of pool. Some of the game variations need tables of special sizes.

Snooker tables. The few snooker tables in the United States are 5 by 10 feet. The pockets are very small, and their corners are rounded rather than pointed as they are on standard tables. Even though the balls used are smaller, it is very difficult to make a shot because of the rounded corners. There are many snooker tables in use in Canada, where the game is very popular, as it is in England and Australia.

Three-cushion billiards tables. The distinctive feature of the table used for three-cushion billiards and some other forms of the carom game is its lack of pockets. There is, therefore, no need to split the rails along the length of the table, so the table has four rails—a long one along each side and a short one along each end. The dimensions are 5 by 10 feet.

LIGHTING

Whatever the style or type of table you play on, it should be placed in a good light. Fluorescent lighting is best; use four 8-foot bulbs. Make sure the light is centered so that there are no shadows and the entire table is illuminated.

BALLS

Years ago, billiard balls were made of clay. Today pocket billiards is played with composition balls made of about 80 percent plastic and 20 percent resin. The *mud balls*, as the old clay ones were called, didn't make as many erratic spins or rolls as the new ones do.

All the balls used in pool games played on full-sized tables are a regulation 2¼ inches in diameter and weigh 5½ to 6 ounces. They're all perfectly round and, except for design, are basically the same. The same size balls would also be used on a 5- by 10-foot or 4- by 8-foot table, but you would use smaller balls (say, 2 inches) if you play on a smaller table, since the pockets are smaller.

If you play in a billiard room there's really no advantage to owning your own set of balls. Balls are standardized, and the ones you find in a billiard establishment are usually kept in good condition. Billiard parlors have ball-cleaning machines, but they're expensive to own and really not necessary to have at home. To keep the balls you have at home in good shape, just wash them off occasion-

BILLIARD BALLS...are a regulation 2¼ inches in diameter. The standard set contains 15 balls plus a white cue ball.

ally with soap and water and then apply a little plastic polish.

A standard set contains 15 balls, numbered 1 through 15, and an all-white *cue ball*, the ball you hit to propel one or more of the balls into a pocket. Balls 1-8 are solid colored and balls 9-15 are striped.

Certain billiards games require special balls. In three-cushion billiards, for example, only three balls are used: a clear white ball, a white ball with a spot, and a red ball. In poker pool, the balls have different colors and are marked to represent playing cards—jack, queen, king, ace. In snooker, the balls are smaller, and there are 15 unnumbered red balls and six balls numbered from 2 through 7.

THE CUE STICK

The *cue stick* is to a good billiards player what a scalpel is to a surgeon, a drill to a carpenter, or a violin to a fiddler. So make sure your cue stick is well made,

properly balanced, and of the right size, and be sure to take care of it.

Even if you play in a billiard parlor rather than on your own table, it pays to own your cue stick because you can select one that's comfortable and use the same cue each time you play. Cues have different weights and thicknesses and, to a degree, slightly different shapes, so it's best to buy the one that's best for you.

Early in the history of billiards, cue sticks were shaped like bats and known as "maces." They were clumsy instruments for striking the ball. Through the years they've become lighter and more thinly tapered.

The standard length of a cue stick is 57 inches, but nowadays good players are breaking away from the standard and starting to use sticks that are 58 or even 58½ inches long. You'd be surprised how often that little extra length eliminates the need to use the *mechanical bridge*. You might take a tip from the pros and buy yourself a longer stick. Even if you're only 10 years old, though, don't use a

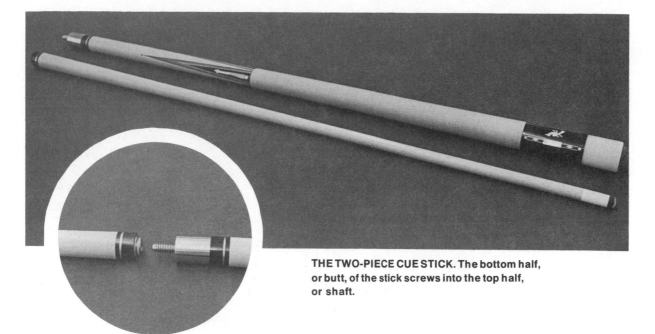

THE TWO-PIECE CUE STICK. The bottom half, or butt, of the stick screws into the top half, or shaft.

stick that's shorter than 57 inches, or you'll have trouble. Learn with the right equipment. I was even younger when I began to use a 57-inch stick.

The circumference of a cue *shaft*, the end of the cue stick with which you hit the ball, varies from 10 to 13 millimeters. The pros use the 13-mm size, and I'd recommend that one to you, especially if you're a beginner, because it provides more hitting surface.

The most important variable of a cue stick is its weight, which you can find stamped in ounces on commercially made cues. There is a tremendous variation in the weights of the sticks. Most professionals use a fairly heavy cue that's between 19½ and 20½ ounces. Some of the pros recommend that you start with a light cue and work up to a heavier cue. But my feeling is that, even if you're young, you should start with a regulation weight if you can handle it comfortably.

Other Cues

There's a big difference between the cue used for straight pool, which we're concentrating on in this book, and the cues used for snooker and carom billiards. The snooker cue has a very thin shaft and weighs between 13 and 15 ounces. The cushion billiards cue is considerably heavier and gets the ball around the table faster. The straight pool cue is between the other two types in weight.

Cue Sections

Cue sticks have two basic sections—the bottom, or *butt*, and the top, or *shaft*. The stick is tapered from the butt to the leather tip at the end of the shaft, with which you stroke the ball.

A cue stick comes in either one or two pieces. If it's in two pieces, the butt has a metal screw at its top that screws into the bottom of the shaft. Aside from making the stick easier to carry—since you can break it into two parts—there is no particular advantage of a two-piece cue stick over a one-piece, since most cues are basically the same style, with leather tip and white *furl*. You'll find that most billiard parlor cues are in one piece and are unjointed and unwrapped. You can buy a customized stick in either one or two pieces from any of about twenty custom cuemakers.

I know players who used to carry around one-piece cues to play with in billiard parlors. The one-piece does have some advantages: once it is seasoned, it's not going to warp or bend, and unlike the two-piece, it has no joint that might swell if it gets wet and no fancy wrapping that can be damaged. But you'd look funny if you rode the bus with a cue stick nearly 6 feet long and walked into a pool hall with it. Some players carry extra shafts for their two-piece cues, so that if anything goes wrong they can replace it.

On the butt end of a two-piece there is usually a wrapping of Irish linen, leather, or nylon. Most of the top pros use linen because it does a good job of soaking up the sweat left by the hand, thus preventing stickiness.

You'll find that wooden cue sticks are much better than aluminum, since they don't reflect temperature changes as much. Also, if you should accidentally strike your wooden stick on the table, it won't bend in half. It might chip, but it won't bend. In a good cue stick, the shaft will be made of maple or another hardwood and the butt will be made of ebony or a similar wood.

All cues are basically the same in design, but workmanship can spell a big difference. If you buy from someone who customizes cue sticks, you know that he's going to take his time making yours and that he'll fit the parts together properly. You certainly don't want the screw in a two-piece cue to be off center; if it is, you have problems. And you don't want anything to go wrong with the wrap.

Try Before You Buy

Before you buy a stick or before you select one to play with in a billiard parlor, try out several by taking practice strokes with them. Your cue should be well balanced so that it has its weight evenly distributed and is not butt-heavy. Trying out cues should also tell you which fits you best as to weight and size. But there are other considerations. While you're practice-stroking, look at the tip to make sure it's solid. This is important. The tip should be about ⅛-inch to ¼-inch high and have a good, rounded shape. The tip's diameter should be 13 millimeters. In three-cushion billiards play, a hard tip is recommended, but for pocket billiards use a medium-hard tip. The wood part of the stick should be free of nicks.

How much should you pay for a cue stick? Well, prices range from about $5 for a one-piece cue to thousands of dollars for a two-piece. I know one man who paid $5,000 for his cue, but that stick had pearls, ivory, diamonds, and everything. The fanciness of your cue isn't going to help your play.

Essentially, the quality of play depends on the player behind the cue stick, no matter whose stick it is. But it helps to have your own cue stick. Jack Nicklaus or Arnold Palmer would play well with my golf clubs or yours, but they'd play better with their own.

Getting back to the price—if you're an average player, you shouldn't pay more than $50 for a two-piece cue. Any cue within the $35 to $200 price range would be a fairly good one that would hold up. But I don't think you should spend more than $200 for your own two-piece cue.

Caring for your Cue

It's important not only to buy a proper

STORING THE CUE STICK. To prevent bending or breaking, store the cue in a rack or place it as flush against the wall as possible. Don't press the cue stick in the middle; it may snap.

cue stick but also to take proper care of it.

When you're storing your stick, it's best to use a standard cue rack. If you don't have a rack, stand the stick as *flush* against the wall as possible. But don't lean the stick against the wall, or you run the risk of putting a bow in the cue.

Wherever you store your cue stick, be sure the temperature isn't extreme or likely to change radically. For example, you should never leave a cue stick in a car overnight. The contrast between the cold of night and the daytime sunshine

beating on the stick can do it a lot of permanent damage.

With a two-piece stick, you should always have a case for protection. The harder the case, the better. If you step on or run over a hard case, the stick inside is more likely to escape damage.

Carrying cases start at about $3 and go up to $50 or $60 or even more for very elaborate ones made of leather or alligator.

When your cue is out of the case, there are several things you can do to keep the stick in tip-top shape. It's a good idea to put some wax on the stick occasionally. I've used a brand name furniture paste wax that really does the job, seasoning the wood and closing up the pores.

The cue should be smooth and clean at all times. For normal cleaning, use a dry rag on the stick every so often. Once in awhile you might want to use a little lighter fluid on a rag to help you close the pores in the wood on your shaft.

A nick in your cue can be very irritating—you'll be aware of it each time you stroke. Many players are tempted to sandpaper their cues to smooth the nick out. Never—*never*—touch the shaft of the cue with sandpaper, because you'll ruin the life of the cue by using the rough foreign element on it. Instead take the stick back to the person who made it and let him take care of it, if the cue is at all valuable. (I do use grade 600A sandpaper to take dirt or caking off my cue stick, but it's such a fine grade, that you can rub your finger with it and hardly feel anything. But you really shouldn't risk using even that.)

THE MECHANICAL BRIDGE
Another piece of equipment sometimes used in pool is the *mechanical bridge*,

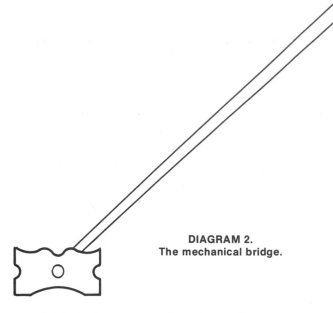

DIAGRAM 2.
The mechanical bridge.

TRIANGLE

Another accessory is a wooden or plastic triangle or rack that enables you to set up the 15 balls in pyramid shape, starting at the foot spot, for various games of pocket pool.

CHALK

One reason you may sometimes *miscue* is that when your cue tip comes in contact with the cue ball there is nothing to grip the tip, so the stick slides off the slippery ball.

Proper chalking will prevent this from happening. The chalk works into the stick and gives it a little bite and grab. Then

which helps you make shots that are out of convenient arm's reach. The mechanical bridge has two parts—a stick, which resembles a cue but is generally a foot longer, and a notched metal plate at right angles to the stick. The notches in the plate are fitted to hold the cue stick, doing the job that your front or *bridge hand* ordinarily would. Since most men can stretch farther than most women, the mechanical bridge is sometimes known as *ladies' aid*. It's also known as a *crutch*.

Although the mechanical bridge is something you're *forced* to use on occasion, I don't consider it a desirable tool. The bridge is difficult to control because it leaves you far away from the ball.

If you do have to use it, make sure you lay it down on the table as flat as possible. Avoid the tendency, common to so many players, of lifting the artificial bridge, because then it's likely to move at the metal end and give you a wobbly, inaccurate stroke. As you hold its handle with your normal bridge hand, grip the cue stick at the end and stroke it as if you're throwing a dart, either with an overhand or sidearm motion.

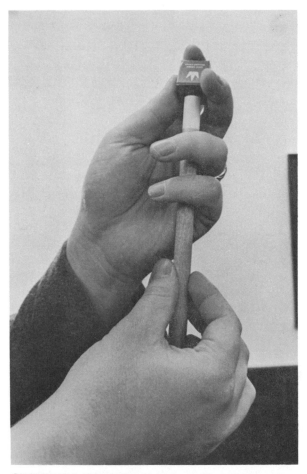

CHALKING A CUE STICK. Hold the chalk on the tip and rotate the stick, not the chalk. Always use a fairly new piece of chalk to avoid getting chalk on the ivory, or furl.

when the stick makes contact with the ball it holds its position.

If the tip is smooth and doesn't take chalk, you can improve its grabbing quality by sandpapering it. Use sandpaper on the tip only when necessary. Sandpapering will also keep the tip from extending beyond the sides and possibly causing miscues. The leather should be kept even with the cue and slightly rounded on the top.

Another way to rough up the tip is to touch it lightly to a file and roll it. Don't use the file in a scraping movement or it will tear your tip. After you've rolled the tip lightly on a file, wet the sides of the tip with a damp cloth and then polish it with either the back of sandpaper or with a smooth piece of leather. This hardens the sides, insures a firm tip, and prevents the tip from spreading.

When you apply chalk, be sure to do it properly. Don't take the chalk cube in your hand and just rub it back and forth as if you're squeezing orange juice from it, something so many players seem to do. The better way is to hold the cube of chalk on the tip of the cue and roll the stick between your palms and fingertips. When you take the chalk cube off, examine the cue tip to make sure you've distributed the chalk evenly. If you've missed a spot, take the edge of the chalk cube and "pencil" in the spots you've missed.

Avoid using a chalk cube that has a deep hole because it's likely that you'll get the chalk only on the sides of the cue and not on the tip where it's vital. Whenever possible, try to use a newer cube. And try to remember to chalk up after every shot or every other one so that you don't miscue.

If you use wet chalk, it won't rub off on your cue tip. Then your opponent could start a run and win the game. There have been times—fortunately, they are rare—when a player has tried to sabotage an opponent's play by wetting his chalk. So inspect your cue to make sure that chalk has stuck to it.

POWDER

If your hands perspire, you'd be wise to apply some powder or resin to them. Don't use too much; just apply a thin coat on your hands so that the cue stick doesn't irritate them as you stroke. Ordinary baby powder is fine for the purpose. In fact, I think it's probably the best thing to use.

THE BRIDGE HAND . . . is the guide to where you will hit the cue ball. Here I'm showing one of my students how to hold his bridge hand so that the bridge is firm and the index finger and thumb pad are in proper position.

chapter 2
THE BASICS

Fundamental to any game played on a pool table are your *stance, bridges, grip,* and *stroke*.

STANCE

The most important thing to remember about your stance is that it has to assure you good balance and allow you freedom of movement for proper stroking. If you're not balanced correctly, your shooting will be erratic. A good thing to do when you've taken your stance is to have someone poke you in the shoulder with his or her index finger. If you lose your balance, you know you're not standing right. Your stance should be firm without being stiff.

Some experts give exact instructions about stance: face the table, stand 10 or 12 inches from it, and place your body in the direction of the shot, with your feet parallel and about as wide apart as your shoulders. Then, they suggest, move your body slightly to the left (if

you're right-handed) so that your right arm and shoulder are lined up with the direction of your shot. Turn your right foot about 45 degrees to the right and bring your left foot around so that it remains parallel to the right but is still about 14 inches apart from it.

It's fine to be this mathematical, but not really necessary. I think you should stand the way you feel best. But why hinder yourself by standing in some awkward, cockeyed position? When Don Carter bowled he held the ball in an unorthodox position, with his wrist twisted and turned in. But how many Don Carters are there? Even when you have to stretch for a shot, it should feel natural.

It all comes back to standing so that you get the most balance. You can't be falling over at the side of the table and still manage to get a smooth stroke with a cue stick. Your feet should be placed in such a way that you can't be knocked over by a strong wind. They should be

WRONG STANCE. Here I'm standing up too straight, which prevents me from getting a good line of sight on the ball.

spread slightly apart, with your weight evenly divided between them. If you're right-handed, hold the cue stick at your right side, with your right hand on the butt and your left hand on the shaft. Face the shot with your left foot forward and slightly turned so that your right arm can swing freely and easily without interference from your body.

It's usually a good idea to bend your front knee slightly and keep the back knee straight. I don't always do this; it depends on the shot I am making. In normal play, you should keep at least one foot on the ground at all times. In some games, it's a foul if you don't.

Don't stand with your body so far back from the table that you've got no stroke.

WRONG STANCE. Here I'm bent over too far and my body is too close to the cue stick, so I can't swing my arm freely.

CORRECT STANCE. My chin is about 10 or 12 inches away from the cue stick, allowing me to sight the ball and move my arm freely. My bridge hand is on the table, 6 to 8 inches from the cue ball. I'm holding the cue stick with my stroking arm about 8 inches from the end of the stick.

A common mistake is keeping the butt of your cue stick even with your body. That's wrong. Your body should be closer to the table than the butt of your cue is.

You can judge when you're at a comfortable distance from the cue ball by placing the cue tip almost on the ball, holding your left arm straight, and holding the butt end of the cue in your right hand at your right hip. Once you feel comfortable, bend your body forward, keeping your eye directly over the cue stick.

Head Over Cue Stick

As to how low your head should lean over the cue stick, different players do well with different styles. Jimmy Moore used to stand almost straight up when he stroked. His erect stance may have been because of his great size—although his arms were not abnormally long—but, in any case, his form was exceptional. At the other end of the spectrum is Cicero Murphy, the black billiards star, who gets his head so far down

MY FEET ARE PARALLEL . . . and at a comfortable distance apart. Notice that my forward leg is slightly bent and my back leg is straight.

TEST YOUR STANCE . . . by having someone push your shoulder. If you find yourself losing balance, you know your stance needs correction.

over his cue stick that the stick almost hits his chin. Luther Lassiter hunches over just slightly. I stand over the cue, neither too erect nor too bent. I agree with Willie Mosconi, who recommends that your head be over the cue, in the line of aim, about 6 or 8 inches from the butt.

BRIDGES

A firm *bridge* is vital to a good game of pocket billiards. Your forward hand (the left one, if you're right-handed) provides the bridge for your cue stick. There are many different types of bridges. Which one you select will depend on such factors as what you find most comfortable, the closeness of the cue ball to the rail,

and whether you have to get over another ball to make contact with the cue ball.

A good distance between your bridge hand and the cue ball is 6 to 8 inches, but it will depend on the circumstances. Too long a bridge allows the tip to sway and increases the danger of missing the particular point you're aiming at on the cue ball.

The best way to make a bridge is to make a fist, placing your fingers knuckle-down on the table and lifting your thumb to create a crevice where you will rest your cue. You don't have to be a contortionist or an acrobat. From this basic position, you can make all sorts of bridges, from one in which your fingers lie flat and extended to one in which your hand rises up, balanced on your fingertips.

When you've gained some experience, you might want to start making a bridge this way. First place your entire hand on the table, with the heel of your hand firmly on the cloth and your fingers extended. Bend your index finger so that the tip of it forms a loop against your thumb. Place the cue in the groove between your thumb and index finger and then through the loop made by your index finger and thumb. Pull your index finger back firmly against the cue.

Some players recommend that you double under the second joint of your middle finger, which, with your other two fingers spreading and pressing firmly against the table, will form a sturdy support with the heel of your hand and your thumb, which are also on the table. The cue passes through the circle of your index finger and is guided by your index finger, thumb, and middle finger.

You can hold the cue stick *closed*, with your index finger curled over it to keep the cue from sliding, or *open*, with the

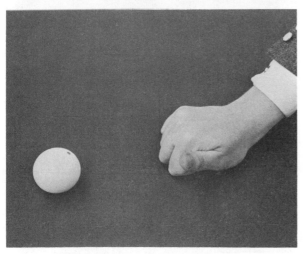

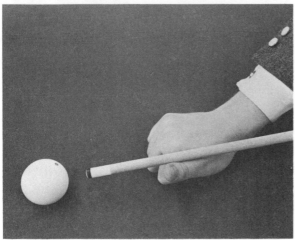

A BEGINNING PLAYER ... should start making a bridge this way. First, place your fist on the table, with your finger knuckles touching the bed of the table. Raise your thumb and place the cue stick between your thumb and index finger.

cue resting on the crease at the base of your thumb, between your thumb and index finger. The closed grip, with the index finger curled over the cue, is most frequently used because the cue stick can't go any place you don't want it to. Professionals tend to use various styles of bridges. You'll find yourself using different ones to meet different situations. For ordinary situations on the table, the open or closed bridges will do equally well.

On a *draw shot*, which we will discuss

THE FLAT OPEN BRIDGE ... is for the more advanced player. From the fist you made, open your fingers and, with your palm on the table, raise your fingers slightly so that your hand bends. Elevate your thumb, cradle the cue between your thumb and index finger, and stroke.

in detail later, you want the cue ball to come back to you after it hits the *object ball*. To make this shot, use a closed bridge. For a *follow shot*, where you want the cue ball to follow the object ball, an open bridge is generally advisable.

To Shoot Over A Ball

Your bridge hand is the guide to where you're going to hit the cue ball. Therefore, to shoot over a ball and elevate the

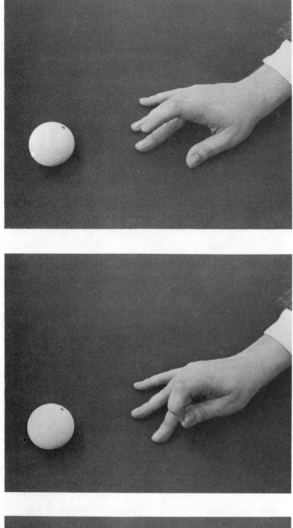

AN EXPERIENCED PLAYER . . . might make a bridge by extending his fingers, raising the thumb and index finger, and placing their pads together. The cue stick fits into the loop made by the thumb and index finger.

cue stick, you should raise the wrist and fingers of your bridge hand rather than raise the butt of the cue. Raising the butt is a common temptation that you should avoid if possible. Similarly, when you want to hit the cue ball low, all you usually have to do is lower your bridge.

When you're shooting over a ball that is between you and the cue ball, it's a good idea to keep your fingers, from their tips to first joints, on the table, pressing on them hard until you feel solid support. Raise your wrist and palm; then curl your thumb above your index finger and stroke the cue stick between them. Some players press hard on the middle and little fingers, with some support by the third finger. Others press their little and index fingers firmly against the table, while the first joints of their middle and third fingers assist.

Before you stroke, make sure the bridge is solid. In hitting over an obstructing ball, it's wise to keep your bridge hand as comfortably close as possible to the cue ball without touching the cue ball with your stick or hand, which constitutes fouling.

Rail Bridges

When the cue ball is close or touching the rail, you have to use a *rail bridge*, a type of bridge in which some or all of your fingers and hand and sometimes the cue rest on the rail. In some rail bridges, your index and middle fingers press gently against either side of the cue and form a slot through which the cue slides.

There are several variations of the rail bridge, depending mainly on how close the cue ball is to the rail. If it's within, say, 6 inches of the rail, the four fingers of your bridge hand should be laid across

THREE RAIL BRIDGES . . . for use when the cue ball is close to the rail but not frozen to it. In the top picture, the thumb is folded under the palm, and the cue stick travels along the thumb and in between the index and middle fingers. In the middle picture, the thumb and index fingers form a loop through which the cue stick slides. The fingers are held on the rail. In the picture on the bottom, fingertips are on the rail and thumb and wrist are raised. The cue fits between the thumb and the index finger. This third bridge is an unsteady one that you should try only if you're an experienced player.

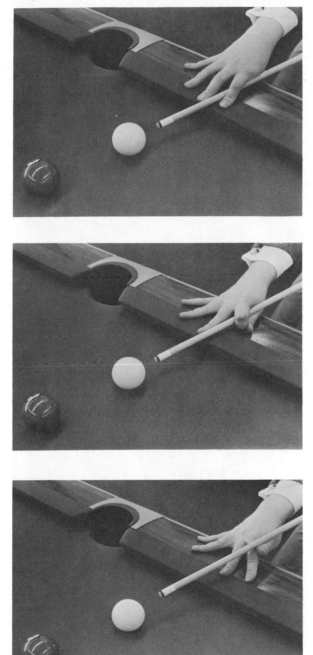

the rail. The cue, which rests on the rail, would then be stroked through the middle and index fingers, with your index finger over the cue and your thumb controlling it from below.

If, however, the cue ball is only an inch or two away from the rail, use the same principle but pull your fingers back from the cushion and let your thumb and index finger give greater control to the cue stick. Do this with your index finger looped around the cue and both your index finger and thumb off the rail. Your thumb should be braced against the outer rail. The cue is stroked along the rail through the loop of the index finger and alongside the middle finger. When the cue ball is right against the rail, or *frozen*, and your shot roughly parallels the rail, you should rest your thumb, your index finger, and part of the heel of your hand on the rail, while your other fingers position themselves on the bed.

There may be times when the cue ball is more than 6 inches from the rail but not far enough away to let you place your entire bridge hand on the table. In this case, the heel of your bridge hand should be rested on the rail, while your fingers and thumb hold the cue stick in the usual way.

Whatever bridge you use, your bridge hand should grasp or otherwise control the shaft of the cue tightly enough so that the stick won't wobble but loosely enough so that it moves smoothly when you stroke. If you notice that the forward motion of your stick is being impeded or stopped by the skin of the index finger curled over it, you know you're holding the cue too tight. Then, obviously, you should relax your hold a bit. If your stroking is proper, the cue stick shouldn't wobble.

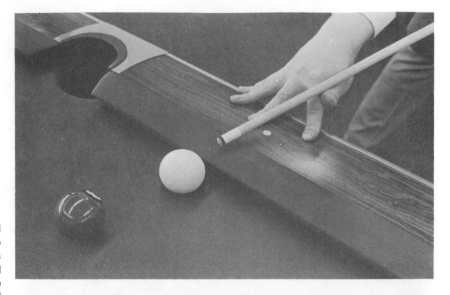

WHEN THE CUE BALL IS FROZEN . . . to the rail, use one of these rail bridges. Top: Place fingers on the rail, with palm down, and raise your thumb. Cradle the cue stick between the thumb and the index finger. The cue stick should slide along the rail, with the thumb and index fingers as guides. Middle: for more experienced players. Place fingers on rail; raise palm and press down on the tips and first joints of your fingers. The cue stick rests on the rail as you stroke. It travels between the thumb and curled index finger and then through the index and middle fingers. Bottom: An unsteady bridge for only very experienced players. Place tips and first joints of finger on rail; bring thumb up and raise wrist; cradle the cue stick between your thumb and index finger.

STROKING PARALLEL TO THE RAIL
... when the ball is against the rail is accomplished by placing the first joints of your middle, ring, and little fingers on the rail. Fold your thumb under your upraised hand and loop your index finger over the cue. Slide the cue stick between the index finger and the rail.

STROKING AT AN ANGLE TO THE RAIL... when the cue ball is frozen. Place your fingers on the rail, fold your thumb under your hand, and stroke, making sure the cue stick is resting on the rail.

THE CUE BALL AND THE OBJECT BALL... are both frozen to the rail. Here are two bridges you can use. Right: Place your middle, ring, and little fingers on the table. Let your index finger rest on the rail; fold your thumb under your palm. Stroke between your index and middle fingers, making sure the cue stick is resting on the rail.

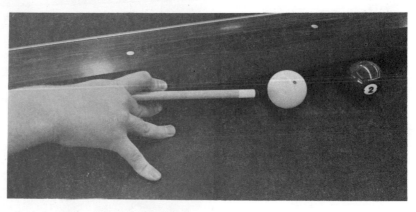

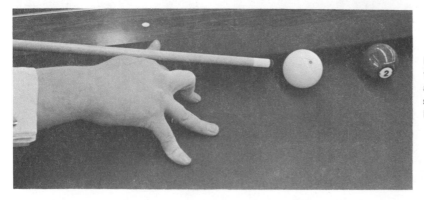

Left: Place your fingers on the table. Rest your hand on the rail and raise your thumb. The cue stick rests in the cradle provided by the thumb.

YOU'RE HOLDING THE CUE IMPROPERLY . . . if you let your index finger overlap your thumb. This position is very unsteady.

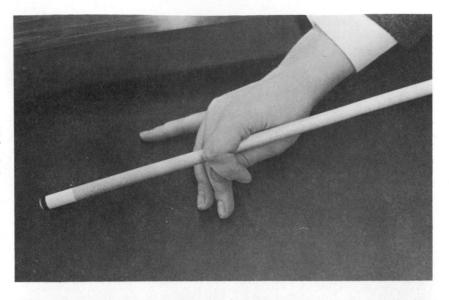

DON'T LEAVE AN OPEN SPACE . . . between the pads of your thumb and index finger. This position doesn't provide a proper resting place for the cue.

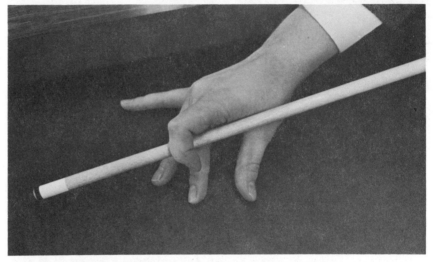

THE CUE STICK HELD CORRECTLY. You should keep the pads of the thumb and index finger together, and the cue stick should flow evenly between the two fingers.

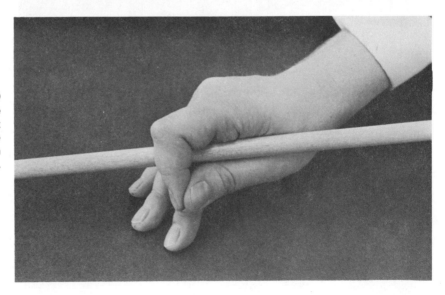

THE WRONG WAY . . . to use a mechanical bridge.
If you raise the bridge, it will become unsteady when
you stroke.

THE RIGHT WAY . . . to use a mechanical bridge. The
bridge hand holds the handle firmly on the table.

Using the Mechanical Bridge

When using the mechanical bridge, remember to keep it as flat as possible on the table. Resist the tendency of many players to raise the bridge, because if you do that, the part of the shaft that is resting on one of the notches of the bridge is going to start moving, spoiling the smoothness and accuracy of your stroke.

To keep the mechanical bridge flat and steady, hold it flat on the table between your middle and index fingers and keep the heel of your hand pressed firmly on top of it. Don't hold it at the very end of the stick.

The bridge should lie to the side of the shot that is away from your power or stroking hand. In other words, if you're right-handed, the artificial bridge should lie to the left of your shot.

To grip the butt of the cue, use a turned-up version of the usual grip. The

cue lies on your thumb with your middle and index fingers on top of the stick.

When using the artificial bridge, sight straight down the cue stick to the cue ball. It's helpful to have the notched head of the bridge a few inches from the cue ball so that you contact the desired point on the cue ball. Which notch or groove you use on the substitute bridge will

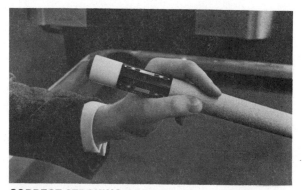

CORRECT STROKING ACTION . . . when using the mechanical bridge comes mostly from the wrist. The cue stick is held between the thumb and index finger.

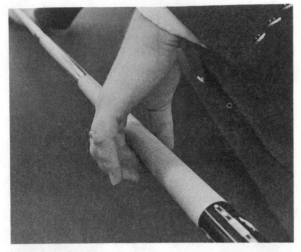

THE WRONG WAY... to grip the cue stick. Don't leave any space between the cue and the skin between your thumb and forefinger, but don't grip the cue too tightly, either.

THE RIGHT WAY ... to grip the cue stick. The cue should be cradled in the palm of your power hand, with the thumb and middle and index fingers gripping it firmly.

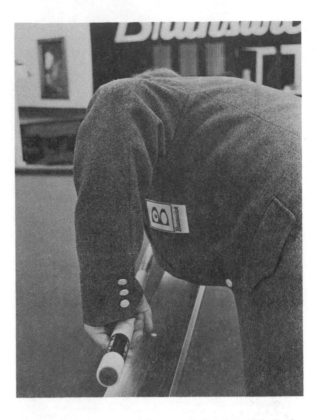

depend on which spot on the ball you want to hit.

GRIP

The power of your stroke comes from the hand that controls the butt of the cue stick. You should grip the cue stick with your *power hand* (your right hand, if you're right-handed) about 6 to 8 inches from the butt end. Some players suggest that you hold the cue stick about 4 inches behind the *balance* of the cue, the point at which the weight of the cue is the same on either side. The butt of the cue should be cradled in the palm of your power hand, with your thumb, index, and middle fingers gripping it firmly and the other two along just for the ride.

Regardless of the situation on the table, you should grip the butt end of the stick in the same fashion. If you find you're doing it differently, there's probably something wrong. You know you're

changing your style, and it shouldn't be done.

It bears repeating: avoid the mistake a lot of players make—lifting the back hand to elevate the cue. When circumstances force you to elevate the stick—either to get over a ball or to try to hit the cue ball low so that it returns—you should if at all possible raise the bridge hand, not the power or stroking hand.

AIMING AT AND SIGHTING THE BALL

Since a billiard table is unlike a golf course, which rolls and turns, you can depend on the cue ball rolling true and straight after you hit it. There's seldom any need to walk around the table to line up a shot from all different angles the way a golfer might do with a putt.

Measure in your mind the angle at which the cue ball will have to hit the object ball in order to drive it into the pocket, and aim for the point you want to contact. Depending on the situation, there will be times when you want the cue ball to hit the object ball squarely or *full ball* and other times when you will want it to strike just a portion of the ball or even barely brush it (*thin ball*). Some pros recommend that you imagine a line drawn from the middle of the pocket through the center of the object ball and that you hit the point on the back of that ball where the imaginary line would come through (Diagram 3). However you arrive at your point of aim, remember: finding the spot isn't difficult; *hitting* it is.

The ability to judge which shot you can make and which shot you should *take* will develop with experience. In straight pool, you should be reasonably sure that you can pocket a ball before calling it. The shrewd player leaves the impossible balls for his opponent.

It's hard to tell you for sure where you should sight first. Probably you'll be looking at the object ball and the pocket simultaneously just before you shoot. Once you've placed your bridge hand on the table and set it in place, it shouldn't move, and your line of aim between cue stick and cue ball should be fixed, so that you don't have to resight as you stroke. You can close one eye when you're sighting, but you need both eyes open when you're shooting.

STROKE

A key point to remember in stroking the ball is that your arm should move only from the elbow down. It should swing like the pendulum of a grandfather's clock—back and forth on a straight plane. Your elbow may move just a hair, but if you lift it you'll be raising the cue

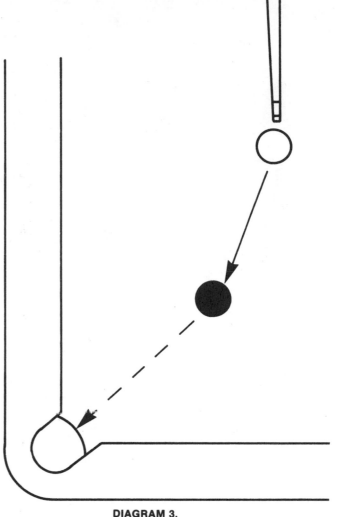

DIAGRAM 3.
Lining up the cue ball with the object ball and pocket.

stick and your stroke will be uneven. Don't move your shoulder either, or you'll be in trouble.

Just keep practicing that pendulum movement until you can feel that you're doing it right. Actually, you can probably see your arm moving, and if you're doing it the right way, you'll be able to tell.

Much of the success of your stroke depends on the wrist action of your power hand. The wrist doesn't act independently; it acts *with* your lower arm. The snap of your wrist should be coordinated with the pendulum swing of your lower arm. As you swing your arm forward, your wrist should whip the cue stick into solid contact with the cue ball. Remember not to grasp the butt of the cue stick too tightly. The wrist should be loose,

AN AWKWARD POSITION. Holding the arm too far away from the body prevents the arm from swinging smoothly.

A good exercise is to place the cue ball about 18 inches from the head of the table and in a direct line with the middle diamonds at the foot and head of the table. Aim at the middle diamond at the foot of the table and try to make the ball return in the same line and hit the end of the cue, which you left in follow-through position. This can be done only if you strike exactly in a vertical line through the ball's center.

Warmup Stroking

No matter what the situation, you should take several practice strokes before you actually make contact with the cue ball. A golfer takes parctice strokes before he putts, and a pitcher will go into a windup motion before he rears back and fires. A pool player has to rear back and fire, too, and you want to make sure your aim and stroke are on the beam.

Some players get up there and—boom!—hit the ball on the first stroke. But you shouldn't. You have to be very conscious of what you're doing. You have to make sure your arm is moving only from the elbow down; you have to make sure your aim is proper. Take your time and stroke the cue three or four times to get in the groove before you take the shot. Too many warmup strokes will tend to make you tired, but too few strokes won't give you sufficient concentration and you won't properly sight the ball.

Your practice strokes should be deliberate, not jerky. After all, you want the warmup strokes to be the same as your actual shot—except, of course, that in your practice strokes you don't make contact with the ball.

Don't vary your preliminary stroking. It's tempting to do one warmup stroke before an easy shot and five before a

not stiff. If you tighten up the wrist, you won't get as good a stroking action as you will if your wrist is flexible.

Most of your stroking action should be wrist action. I know several players who put just about their entire bodies into their swings. This will give more power to your stroke, but it's unnecessary. The reason Hank Aaron hits a baseball so terrifically isn't because he's brutally powerful—he isn't—but because he's got very strong wrists and he knows how to coordinate them. The same principle applies to you and your pool-playing. You need a good wrist, well coordinated with your power arm.

As in hitting a baseball, you need a backswing before striking a cue ball. Bring your cue stick back a distance equal to the length of your bridge and let fly with a quick, level shot.

tough one. But you should take the same number of strokes before every shot, regardless of how easy or difficult the shot appears to be. I've seen *hangers*—where the object ball is "hanging" right near the pocket—missed by the best of players. It usually happens because they rushed into the shot. I've done it myself several times. Once in Chicago I was playing Frank McGowan and had a shot that was so simple a baby could have made it. The shot was worth a couple of thousand dollars in prize money. I just got up and hit it. The ball ricocheted back and forth from one side of the pocket to the other and then hung right there on the lip of the pocket. Luckily for me, the cue ball caromed off the rail and put my opponent behind a cluster of balls where he didn't have a clear shot at the ball hanging on the lip. He banked the cue ball but missed the object ball completely. So it was my turn again. Needless to say, this time around I took all the time in the world. I went to the table, went back, put powder on my hands, took a drink of soda, got a towel, wiped my brow, and finally went back to the table and—after some warmup strokes—made my shot. I won the match, but I almost had heart failure because of my hasty carelessness. It taught me a lesson I'll never forget: take practice strokes, no matter how easy the shot. Hangers are missed sometimes. But they shouldn't be and wouldn't be if players took some preliminary strokes to get in the groove.

Whether you play a deliberate or a speedy game, take those warm-up strokes. Your final stroke will be faster than your warmup as a result of the quick snap of your wrist.

Each player has his or her own pace. I play pretty quickly; I'm not deliberate.

As a rule, the quicker I go the better I play and the fewer mistakes I make. Eddie Robin, the three-cushion billiards ace, has a different approach. "I know many consider me a slow player," he told *Billiard Review*. "That's OK. Because when I get up to the table for a certain shot I have to know that everything else is put aside. I want everything other than that one shot out of my mind."

The speed with which you stroke will determine the action of the cue ball, not only before it hits but also after it makes contact with an object ball or cushion. The speed of your stroke should be uniform throughout the game, no matter what kind of shot you're taking.

The intensity of your stroke is another matter. If you just want to nudge the object ball into the pocket, or if you want the cue ball to hit only one cushion, you naturally will hit it a lot more gently than if you want the cue ball to carom off nine cushions.

In any situation, you've got to hit the ball as if you mean it. Hit with some authority—with speed and solidity. You can't baby a ball, or your cue stick will probably swivel and your stroke will be soft and ineffectual. On the other hand, you don't want to hit the ball so hard that you lose control.

How much force an object ball receives is determined by the point of impact with the cue ball and the speed of the stroke.

Exactly how hard you will want to hit the cue ball will depend on your touch and on the feel and judgment you develop with practice. Keep practicing grooving your swing—coordinating your wrist and arm action.

Follow-Through

As in any other sport, the follow-through

HITTING THE BALL DEAD CENTER . . . is essential when you first start playing pool. Most of your shots will be hit this way.

in billiards is very important. You don't want to start looking up or lifting your cue stick before you've hit the ball solidly. To prevent your stick from striking the cue ball at a spot higher or lower or more to the side than you want, follow through with your stroke. Stay down in position and keep your cue stick on the table as long as reasonably possible after the shot. That includes keeping your bridge hand in position, too. Otherwise you're likely to twist your body and spoil the accuracy of your shot.

Finish your stroke with the cue tip a few inches past where the cue ball rested. Don't let your cue tip waver around in the air after you deliver your stroke.

SPECIAL SHOTS

Most of the time you'll want to hit the cue ball in the center. There's less chance of your cue tip slipping off, and a ball

FOLLOW. To make a cue ball follow the object ball after it makes contact, hit the cue ball above center.

struck in the center rolls truer. But under special circumstances, because you want your cue ball to react in a particular way, you'll deliberately hit the cue ball off-center. These off-center shots have different names and purposes: *follow*, *draw*, and *English*.

Follow

If you want the cue ball to move forward after it strikes the object ball, you should hit it above center with a level cue and follow-through. This shot is called *follow* because the cue ball will spin forward and follow in the direction of the object ball. Never hit the cue ball at the extreme top, because there's too much risk of miscuing. Try to keep your bridge hand at a point that enables you to keep your cue level. Hitting the ball too high also spoils accuracy and desired action of your shot.

Draw

A *draw shot* is used when you want to "draw" the cue ball back toward you after it makes contact with the object ball.

A DRAW SHOT . . . is used to keep the cue ball from following the object ball into the pocket. If you execute this shot correctly, hitting the cue ball just below center, the cue ball will come back toward you.

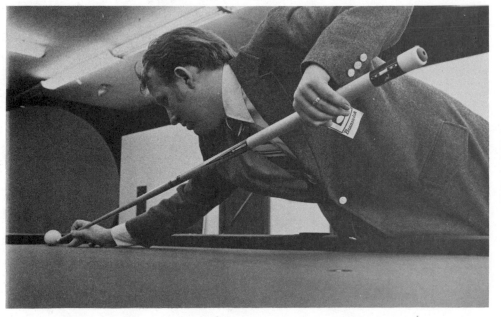

DON'T RAISE THE CUE . . . to hit the cue ball below center on the draw shot. Keep the cue level and lower your bridge instead.

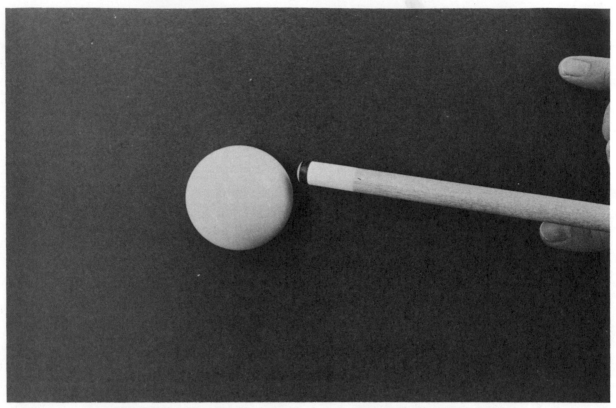

RIGHT-HAND ENGLISH. The ball will spin to the left and then curve to the right.

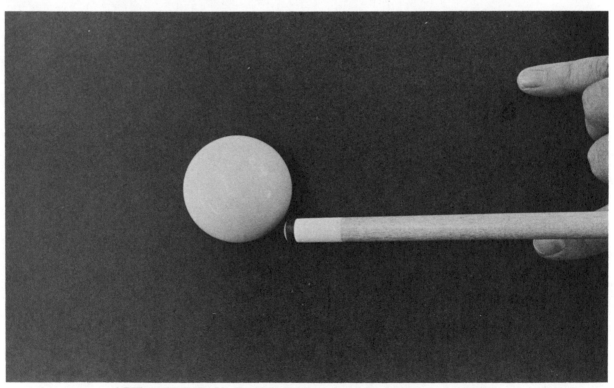

LEFT-HAND ENGLISH. The ball will spin to the right and then curve to the left.

You make a draw shot by hitting the cue ball below center with your cue level and by following through. The lower you hit the ball, the more draw you're likely to get, although other factors—how hard you hit and how fast—will also affect the amount of draw. Don't hit it at the extreme bottom. And no matter what type of shot you're hitting—draw or follow—follow straight through.

Hitting the cue ball hard, fast, and low will result in the greatest amount of draw. There *may* be times when it is necessary to elevate the butt of your cue to draw a shot successfully—for example, if the cue ball is near the rail or if you have to stroke over an object ball. When lifting the butt is necessary, picture the horizontal axis of the cue ball as being at the same angle as the elevation of your cue, and strike the ball below the axis. Otherwise, just hit the cue ball below center, with the stick as level as possible.

Sticking the Cue Ball

It's possible to hit the cue ball in such a way that it stops dead in its tracks after it hits the object ball. This stop action is sometimes known as *sticking* the cue ball.

Sticking is a difficult trick to accomplish on a table with a new cloth, but usually all it takes is a stroke a little below the center of the cue ball (not as low or as hard as you'd stroke to "draw"). How far below center you should hit it will depend on how far away you are from the ball. When you're close to the ball you don't have to hit it quite as much below center. But be sure to hit the ball only at a normal rate of speed. Excess speed will make the ball draw back; you want it to stick.

English

English is a spinning motion created by hitting the cue ball to the left or right of center. The motion affects not only the cue ball when it comes into contact with an object ball or cushion but also the course of the first object ball, which will spin in the direction opposite that of the cue ball.

If you hit the cue left of center, the cue ball will spin to the right and curve to the left. This is called *left-hand English*. The opposite is called *right-hand English*.

If you're ever going to be an accomplished pool player, English is something you'll have to master. But you can get into more trouble applying English improperly than if you don't use it at all. So use as little English as possible. When you do use it, your stroke can't be rigid; it's got to be sharp and springy. You have to follow through. And you have to allow for the curved path a ball takes when English has been applied.

According to most experts, you can apply English on 99 percent of all billiard shots by striking the cue ball only the width of a cue tip from the center of the ball. Going wider than that point to either side increases the chances of miscuing.

There are two basic kinds of English —*natural* and *reverse* (See Diagram 4.)

Natural English, sometimes called *running English*, is applied to the side of the cue ball toward which you want it to travel after it hits the object ball or cushion. In other words, a cue ball hit to the left of center will travel left after it hits a ball or cushion.

Reverse English is applied to the side of the cue ball that is *opposite* the direction you want it to travel after it hits an object ball or a cushion.

Natural English adds speed to the cue ball after it hits a cushion and widens the angle of the ball caroming off the

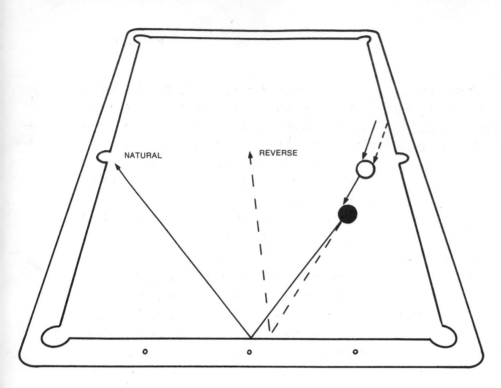

NATURAL   REVERSE

DIAGRAM 4.
The types of English. The drawing
above shows the difference between
reverse and natural English. The
drawing on the right shows where
the ball travels when left-hand and
right-hand English are used.

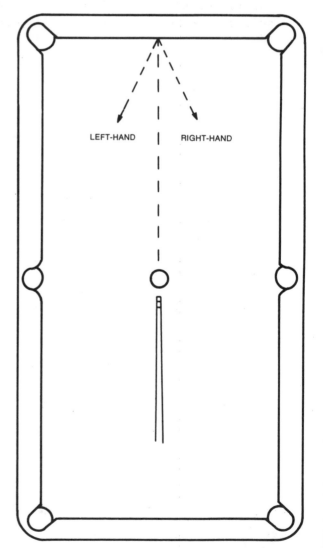

LEFT-HAND   RIGHT-HAND

cushion.

Reverse English does the opposite. It slows the ball's speed, narrows the angle, and actually reverses the course the cue ball would normally travel after striking a cushion.

Curve

As mentioned above, if you apply natural English to the cue ball on the right, it will spin counterclockwise (left) but curve to the right. The longer the shot, the wider will be the arc of this curve. When you're planning your shot, you must take into account what the path of that curve is likely to be.

For example, on a table-length shot, if you want to barely touch the object ball on its left side, a left-English shot might curve too much and miss the object ball. So you would estimate the curve and compensate by aiming to hit more of the object ball. In other words, you have to allow for the amount of curve the cue ball will take and hit it according to the degree of cut you want the object ball to have.

There are different degrees of English you can create. The more spin you want, the harder you hit the ball.

At times you'll want to combine English with either draw or follow. In any event, you should devote a good deal of practice to perfecting each one of these techniques, for how well you master them will determine how well you play position—the mark of a good pocket billiards player.

A PRACTICE DRILL . . . for position play consists of putting all the balls in a circle and placing the cue ball inside the circle. You should try to pocket all the balls while making sure that the cue ball touches only the specific object ball and does not touch the rail.

The game played in billiard champion-ships is *14.1 continuous pocket billiards*, a form of straight pool that requires all-around playing skill. If you learn to play 14.1 you'll be able to play *any* pocket billiards game, so let's talk about play-ing strategy, special situations, and pitfalls.

The object of 14:1 is to score a specific, predetermined number of points before your opponent does. In friendly games, you can set any point total as the winning score—say, 50 or 100 points. In cham-pionshiop play, 150 is the customary total. The game is sometimes known as *call shot*, because in order to score, you've got to designate the object ball at which you're aiming and the pocket into which you intend to drop it. You get one point for every ball you hit into a designated pocket. You also get a point for any ball pocketed along with a legal shot. The game is played with a cue ball and 15 object balls numbered from 1

through 15. In 14:1, each ball is worth a point.

At the start of the game, the cue ball is *in hand*—that is, placed anywhere between the head string and the head of the table—and the numbered balls are set in a triangle at the foot of the table. The 15-ball is placed on the foot spot at the head of the triangle, the 1-ball goes at the rear left corner, and the 5-ball is placed at the rear right corner. The player who opens drives the cue ball into one or more of the balls in the rack.

THE OPENING BREAK

One of the most important shots of any game played on a pool table is the *opening break*, the shot in which the racked-up balls are broken apart at the beginning of the game. That shot can make or break your game.

In baseball, the other team always gets a chance at bat. In tennis, your opponent always has a shot at returning your serve. But billiard games are one form of competition in which one player can win without allowing his opponent a turn. So you can see why the break is so important.

If you are the player to break in the game of *one pocket*, where you're trying to put the balls near your pocket, or in *nine ball*, where you might make the winning ball on the break, or in *rotation*, where you're trying to pocket a ball, it would definitely be to your advantage. But in 14.1, where the chance of making a called shot on the break is so slim and the likelihood of setting up easy shots for your opponent is so great, it is definitely *not* to your advantage to break.

To decide who breaks, you and your opponent can flip a coin, choose, or do what the pros do—*lag*. To lag, you each take a turn shooting the cue ball down the side rail to the foot rail, trying to bring it back as close to the head rail as possible. The player who comes closest to the head rail has the option of whether to break. Remember: if you win the toss or lag, you can request your opponent to break.

In the 1920s, two nervous opponents in an 18.2 balkline carom championship—Jake Schaefer, Jr., and Erich Lagenlacher—each wanted his opponent to break. They both lagged poorly, and the lag was awarded to Schaefer, who proceeded to break and run a world-record 400 for the title. His opponent never got a chance to shoot. Schaefer admitted that he had lagged badly on purpose so that his opponent would have to start the game. Hagenlacher had done the same, also because he wanted Schaefer to shoot first. "A world title at stake," commented Willie Hoppe, "and neither one of these great players knew,

or else entirely overlooked, the fact that one winner of the lag has the *option* of shooting first or requesting his opponent to take the opening shot."

The particular game and your game strategy will determine where to place your cue ball, the force with which you hit the cue ball, the spot on the cue ball at which to aim your cue stick, and the section of the rack of balls at which you aim.

There are also rules that affect the way you break. For instance, in 14.1 and other games of straight pool, you must drive two or more of the object balls in addition to the cue ball to a cushion or put an object ball into a pocket. If you do neither on the break, you scratch. This is one reason that it's to your advantage for your opponent to break.

If you are the one who has to break, remember that a good break will leave your opponent with either no shot or with a tough one.

A good way to break in 14:1 is to set your cue ball along the head string, to the side you find more comfortable. I put the cue ball to the right and, using right-hand English, try to clip just about a quarter of the ball in the rear righthand corner of the triangle. I hit the cue ball just right of the middle to give it right-hand English, so that the cue ball will bounce off the rear cushion at one of the diamonds, hit a side rail at a diamond near the foot of the table, and then hit a diamond on the opposite side of the table.

If you're lucky, you won't leave your opponent with any decent shot. When it's your turn again, if you have a choice between hitting a close shot and a distant one, take the one that's nearer. It's almost always the easier shot. If you're a more advanced player, you might, for reasons of position, take the more distant.

The player who opens doesn't usually call a ball and pocket because the chances of making the shot is so unlikely. On the opening break, if a ball that wasn't called goes in, it's *spotted* and you're not credited with a score.

MISSES

A *missed shot* is an error that ends your inning. There's no penalty if you fail to make the cue ball contact the designated object ball, providing the cue ball hits at least one other ball and drives it into a cushion or a pocket or the cue ball hits a cushion after hitting an object ball. If you fail to do either, you lose a point as well as your turn.

Object balls that are pocketed illegally are spotted on the foot spot. If that spot is occupied, the next ball is put directly behind it on the (imaginary) *long string*.

THE BEST DEFENSE

The best defense in pocket billiards is a good offense, primarily because of the peculiar nature of the game—the fact that one player can win without his or her opponent ever getting a shot. I've won and lost games in which this has happened.

This is not to say that you never play defensively. There are times when you should play a *safety*, a shot you deliberately take to leave the balls safe, or *tough* for your opponent, with no attempt or intention of making a point. In other words, you more or less sacrifice your turn and leave your opponent with what you hope is an impossible shot. You would do this when you're in a very tough situation, when you don't have a shot that you can make, or when you lack the confidence that you can make any shot open to you. Most of the time you want to be careful that you don't *scratch* and

lose a point. But there are circumstances when you'll decide it's worthwhile to lose the point rather than to set your opponent up for an easy shot that could trigger a long run.

When your opponent is off on a long run, your only "defense" is to pray that the table will collapse or that he or she will be struck by a thunderbolt before *running out* (winning). The fact is that once your opponent gets started you can't do anything about it. The trick is to prevent your opponent from getting started by playing sharp defense.

I've seen championships won with a high run of only 54 balls, a very low figure. This probably testifies to the smart defensive play of both competitors. Sometimes, we'll run 150 balls (the maximum, when you play the game to 150 points). I've gone as high as 285 in an exhibition, and others have done better than that, but sometimes you're better off to shun the big run for defensive reasons. A big run is nice, but a consistent 50 or 60 is much better than an occasional 100.

POSITION PLAY

No matter what your playing level, you should always take the shot you think you think you can make. If you're a beginning player, always take the easiest shot first. Do your light work before you take on the heavy tasks, and don't overly concern yourself with position. As you develop your skills, however, you should think more about position and making the shots that will follow the one you're attempting now. When I'm playing well, I'll take a semitough shot to get into position for the next ball. When I'm playing poorly, I don't have confidence about making the fairly tough shot, so I'll go for the easy ones. But that's really not the way an advanced player should approach the game.

All that position involves is planning ahead, trying to pick your next shot or shots. When all 15 balls are on the table, look only one or two shots ahead. But when you get down to, say, five balls, you should decide the order in which you intend to play all five and position your cue ball on each shot accordingly.

On break shots, or when you are trying to break up a cluster of balls, you can't play position because you don't know what's going to happen. Here's where the element of luck plays a big part. Once you've scattered the balls, you can try position play.

The key thing to remember is that in position play you're trying not only to pocket your object ball but also to have your cue ball located in such a position after the shot that you have clear sailing to make the next object ball.

To improve your position play, practice these two exercises:

1. Line up the balls in a circle in the middle of the table, with the cue ball in the center. Try to make every single ball without missing and without letting the cue ball touch a rail. If it hits a rail, you've lost. To do this exercise, you're going to have to call all your billiards skills into play: draw, follow, and English.

2. Place a ball at the foot spot and form a large "L" with all the other balls. Then, with the cue ball anywhere outside the "L," try to pocket all the balls in the corner pocket, starting with the ball closest to the rail.

PUTTING ALL THE BALLS IN THE "L" . . . into the corner pocket is a good drill for practicing position play.

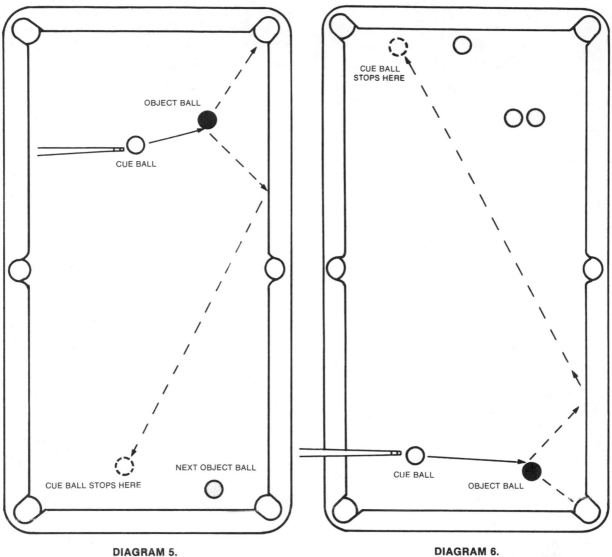

DIAGRAM 5.
Stroke the cue ball to the right of center, so that it will carom off the rail and be in position for the next shot.

DIAGRAM 6.
Hit the cue ball to the left of center, so that it will carom off the rail and be in position for the next shot.

To help yourself in position play, try to hit the smallest number of balls possible on one shot.

When you scatter a cluster of balls, don't scatter them too hard. You want all the balls within the same half of the table. You should try to play in the four pockets that are at the middle and foot rails of the table rather than in all six pockets, because you don't want to have to be shooting your cue ball up and down the table. Imagine a line across the middle spot and do your best to work from there to the foot. If any balls go up to the other end, try to pick them off as soon as possible. Diagrams 5, 6, 7, 8, and 9 show how I would approach some common pool situations. Study these diagrams to get some idea of how to play position.

TROUBLE BALLS

No matter how well-planned your

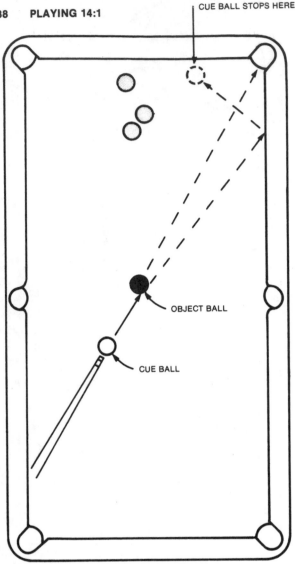

DIAGRAM 7.
To be in position for the next shot, the cue ball
must follow the object ball.

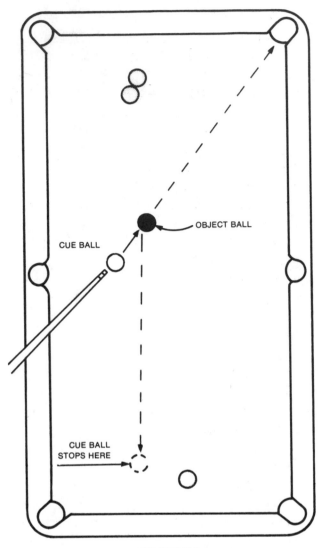

DIAGRAM 8.
To be in position for the next shot, the cue
ball must come back toward you after it hits the
object ball. Make a draw shot by striking the cue
ball below center.

strategy may be, you'll occasionally be confronted with *trouble balls*, balls clustered together near a rail, away from the rack at the foot of the table, or in some other location in such a way that they loom as trouble. Try to clear these off first. If you're an advanced player, you might hit your cue ball so that while pocketing an object ball the cue ball knocks the trouble ball into a rail and out of your way. Or you might try to pocket the trouble ball. Even if you have to alter your game plan, break up those trouble balls, or later in the game they'll give you exactly that. (Diagrams 10 and 11.)

Because you want to avoid unforeseen problems, if you're an experienced player you usually will try to avoid having your cue ball graze any ball other than the one you're trying to pocket. The ball you

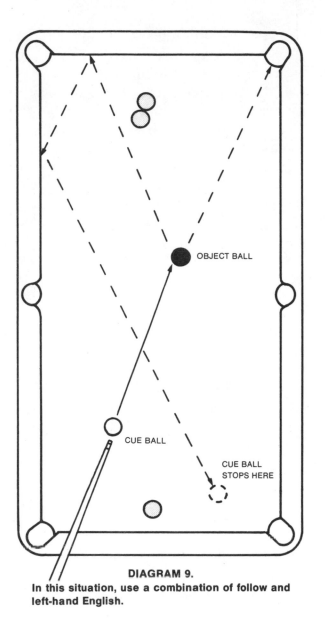

DIAGRAM 9.
In this situation, use a combination of follow and left-hand English.

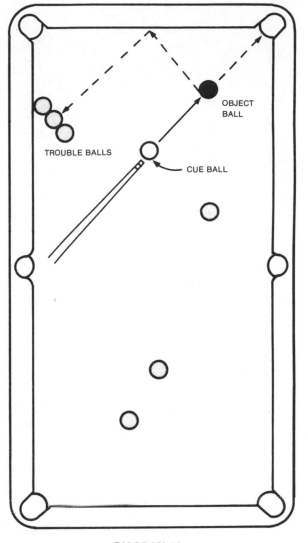

DIAGRAM 10.
In this situation, I would pocket the object ball and have the cue ball carom off the lower rail and break up the cluster of three balls.

graze is liable to come into the path of your next shot and destroy your strategy. Also, you have little idea of where the cue ball will go if it should accidentally graze another ball.

In dealing with trouble balls you must try to control that ever-present element of luck. You want to be able to just go "bing" and pocket your object ball according to plan. You don't want to take a chance on what your next shot is going to be, and you don't want to have to break open anything when you're getting set to go off on a run. So get rid of those trouble balls as soon as possible and leave yourself clear for execution of your game plan.

SCRATCHING

A *scratch* is a miss or a shot that usually

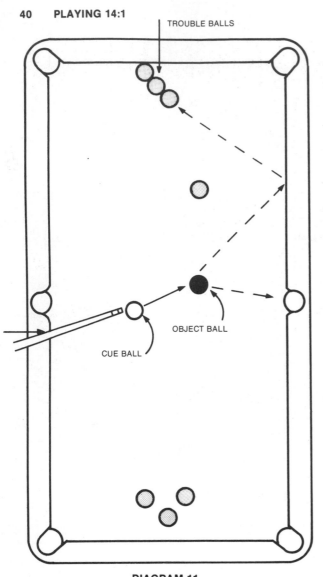

TROUBLE BALLS

OBJECT BALL

CUE BALL

DIAGRAM 11.
In this situation, I would pocket the object ball in the side pocket. I'd do this by using English and hitting the ball on its left side. The cue ball should carom off the side rail and break up the cluster of balls lying on the foot rail.

results in a penalty. It occurs in several different ways.

If you hit the cue ball into a pocket in straight pool games such as 14.1, you lose a point and a ball is taken out and placed on the foot spot. If the cue ball follows your object ball into the pocket, the point you would have received for pocketing your object ball is nullified. In that case, both balls are respotted—the

object ball at the foot spot or right behind a ball that is already there, the cue ball anywhere behind the head string.

If the cue ball jumps off the table, it's a scratch and a one-point penalty. In championship play, the same rules apply to an object ball that goes off the table. In games other than championships, an object ball that jumped off the table would be spotted at the foot string without loss of a point. Your inning or turn would end, though, as it does with any scratch.

Failure of your cue ball and two other balls to hit a rail on the opening break in straight pool games is also a scratch, as noted. You also scratch anytime your cue ball fails to hit another ball or if both your cue ball and an object ball fail to hit a rail (unless a ball is pocketed).

Rules relating to scratching vary with the particular game. In nine ball, for instance, a scratch brings only the end of your shot, while in 14.1 or any other straight pool game, it's both a penalty and the end of your inning.

There are several ways of preventing your cue ball from following an object ball into the pocket, even on an easy straight-in shot. A draw shot, hitting the cue ball below center to make the cue ball stop, is one way. But even if you hit the cue ball dead center, it shouldn't go in. You can prevent the cue ball from going into the pocket by not hitting it very hard and by hitting it so that it glances off the object ball at a slight angle.

If your cue ball is lined up straight with the pocket, hit the object ball a little to one side, so that the cue doesn't follow it in. If you want to hit the object ball in the middle, make sure that you hit the cue ball low to bring it back (draw).

If the object ball is at an angle, rather than lined up straight between your cue ball and the pocket, use your judgment

I MIGHT MAKE AN INTENTIONAL FOUL . . . in a situation such as this one, in which I would have little chance of making the shot.

A BALL HANGING NEAR THE EDGE . . . of a pocket should not be hit squarely, because the cue ball would follow the object ball into the pocket. Draw the cue ball, or have it clip the object ball at an angle. In this case, I recommend clipping the object ball rather than drawing the cue ball.

POSITION PLAY. When balls are spread out from one end of the table to another, clear the head of the table first, then work your way down to the rack area.

14:1 IS CONTINUOUS . . . because, after 14 of the object balls are pocketed, they are reracked. The 15th ball becomes the break ball. In this break shot, a corner pocket break shot, I will strike the cue ball, put the object ball into the corner pocket, and also break open the cluster of balls for the next shot.

and hit the cue ball off to the side that's away from the pocket.

How hard you should strike the cue ball will depend on how far away you are from the object ball and whether or not you're playing position.

Scratching Deliberately

As you develop your playing skill, there will be times when you'll want to scratch *deliberately* rather than risk setting up your opponent for a long run on an open table. This is a part of defensive play, which figures so importantly in pocket billiards.

If you scratch—deliberately or not —you lose a point. If you scratch three times consecutively, you are penalized an extra 15 points, for a total of 18 points. It's a burden to start with minus-18, but it may still give you more of a protective advantage than, let's say, opening with a break that scatters the balls all over and gives your opponent wide-open shots.

The same might apply whenever you're confronted with a tough situation—when you don't have a shot you can make or when there is a shot but you don't have confidence that you can make it. In that case you should figure, Why do the job for my opponent? Let your opponent break the cluster of balls open.

Sometimes I've beaten a player 150 to minus-25 because he'd taken three deliberate scratches in a row, plus some others, during the game. But since this is one competition where you can win without your opponent getting a turn, the fellows I beat by these minus scores figured it was better to take the gamble and sacrifice points early in the game than set me up for a potentially winning run

of balls. Even though it didn't work out, it was the right strategy.

Actually, I don't recommend this outside of championship play. If I were you, I would never take more than one or two scratches in a row.

KEY BALL AND BREAK BALL

What makes the game of 14.1 continuous is that after 14 of the object balls have been pocketed, the 15th ball stays on the table as the *break ball*. The 14 pocketed balls are then racked up, and the game continues.

Your chances of running up a high score or *running out*—winning the game—depend on whether you can keep going through the transition from one or two balls left on the table to when they're reracked and all 15 are in play.

The key to how well you're progressing in pool often lies in how you handle the *key ball*, the next-to-last ball on the table before you rerack.

A good player will decide when several balls are left which of these is going to be the break shot and which one will be the key shot and will maneuver accordingly. If you're capable of making the decision, pocketing the key shot, and getting into excellent position for the break shot, you're on your way to becoming a good player. See Diagram 12 for an example of this type of planning.

Which ball is your break ball is usually fairly obvious. For one thing, you'll want it to be one that is relatively close to where the triangle of balls will come, because, as you know, the farther your cue ball has to travel, the tougher the shot will be.

Continue making the ball outside the triangle. Your strategy is to pocket the break ball in a pocket that you call and

A BEHIND-THE-RACK BREAK SHOT . . . is not recommended because your cue ball can get tied up in the cluster of balls and leave you without a good next shot.

SET UP THE BEST POSSIBLE BREAK SHOT . . . by trying to draw the cue ball back toward the center of the table.

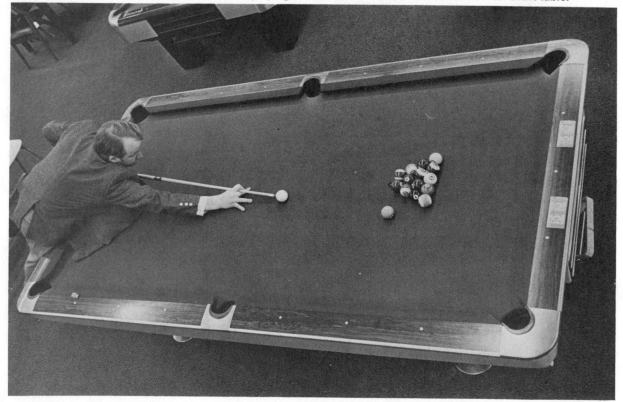

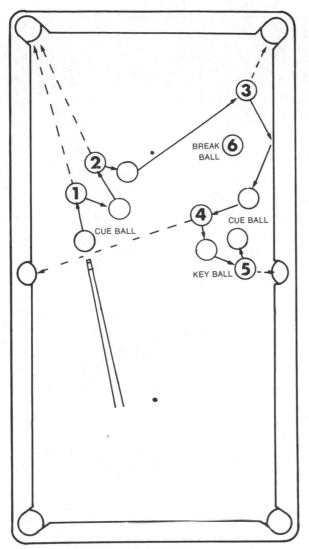

DIAGRAM 12.
When you pocket ball 1, draw the cue ball back to the right. Pocket ball 2 and use a stop position. Pocket the third ball and draw the cue ball along the rail so that the fourth ball can be pocketed. Use the stop position and then pocket the fifth ball.

have the cue ball carom from the break ball into the triangle of racked balls. You can also carom the cue ball from the break ball into one or more cushions and then into the rack.

You don't *have to* shoot at the break ball. You continue until you miss or scratch or until you score the required number of points for the game.

If the last ball on the table is left within the perimeter of the triangle where the other balls are to be reracked, that ball is spotted on the head spot. If the cue ball and unpocketed object ball interfere with the racking of the 14 balls, all 15 object balls are reracked. If the cue ball interferes with the racking of the balls, one of two things happens: if the break ball is outside of the head string, the cue ball is in hand and you can place it anywhere behind the head string for the break. If the break ball is *within the head string* (in the area between the head string and the head of the table), the cue ball is placed on the head spot. If the break ball happens to be there, it is moved to the center spot to allow the cue ball to be placed on the head spot.

Whatever the situation, if you decide to shoot into the rack rather than at the break ball, you've got to either pocket a ball, drive an object ball to a cushion, or make the cue ball hit a cushion after contacting an object ball.

RUNS

The ability to deal with the break shot is more important than being able to get on a high run. You can't manage a high run without being able to make the break shot.

High runs are interesting to fans—and to players, of course, since prizes are sometimes given for them . . Willie Mosconi once pocketed 526 balls in a row in an exhibition. But you can win matches without any very high runs. As I mentioned, I know a man who won a major tournament championship with a high run of only 54.

You are improving very well if, after six months of play, you can run 15 balls in a row, because that means you made 14 and when the balls were reracked you maneuvered yourself into position to

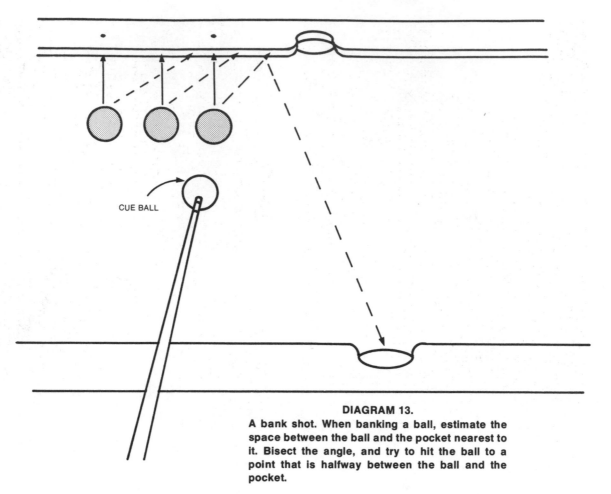

CUE BALL

DIAGRAM 13.
A bank shot. When banking a ball, estimate the
space between the ball and the pocket nearest to
it. Bisect the angle, and try to hit the ball to a
point that is halfway between the ball and the
pocket.

make the break shot. Actually, that's a terrific accomplishment. If you can make 15 it means you can conceivably run 30 or 45.

There are some new players who are naturals—they're running 30 or 40 a couple of months after they start playing. I had a high run of something like 58 when I was seven years old. Those are the exceptions. Luckily, so are the players who never do more than two in a row.

A more important indication of your progress, though, is in pocketing the ball. If you can make a difficult shot, there's hope for you. Above all, if you've got a feel for the game and you really like it, you'll develop into a good player.

BANKS AND CAROMS
If you're a beginner, you're going to find

it's hard enough to make a ball go straight. So don't go after a *carom* shot, where you ricochet the cue ball off one object ball and into another, or a *bank* shot, where you drive the object ball into one or more cushions before pocketing it (Diagram 13.)

These shots are flashy and challenging, but very, very difficult. So wait until you're an advanced player before attempting them.

Bank shots are tough because of the difficulty you have in judging the angle at which the object ball is going to leave the cushion. Often the angle will increase as the speed of the object ball decreases.

There are different types of carom shots. The most common is the one in which you carom the cue ball off a first

A BANK SHOT. After the cue ball hits the object ball, the object ball will carom off the rail and into the pocket at the corner where I am standing.

A KISS SHOT. I will stroke the cue ball into the object ball, which will carom off the other ball and into the pocket.

object ball and into a second with the second object ball pocketed. In another shot, you carom one object ball off a second and that *first* object ball then proceeds to the pocket.

In the game of *rotation*, you may be forced into a carom shot because your object ball has to be a particular one, and it may be hidden from your cue ball by other balls. One pocket is another story entirely. In that game, carom shots are a major part of the offense. Basically, your opponent isn't going to leave you with a clear shot, so you'll have to bank. But you've got to be very skilled to do it. In other games, don't bank or carom unless there's absolutely no alternative. You'll have to carom or bank, for example, when you're *snookered*—when

there are one or more balls between the cue ball and the object ball you want to pocket in such games as rotation.

A kiss, as a carom is sometimes called, may be a desirable smack on the lips, but in pocket billiards, where it refers to one ball glancing off another, it's not always pleasurable. Sometimes you'll want a ball to kiss another for purposes of position and you'll shoot for it to happen. But at other times a kiss will occur by accident and the balls may become frozen—touching a rail or one another—in a way that creates problems for you on your succeeding shots (see Diagram 14, for example).

COMBINATIONS
A *combination shot* involves driving your cue ball into one or more object balls,

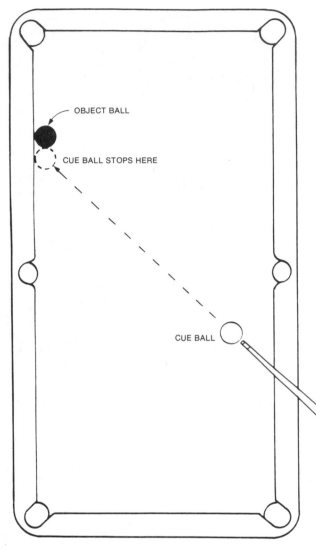

OBJECT BALL

CUE BALL STOPS HERE

CUE BALL

DIAGRAM 14.
When the object ball is frozen to a cushion, strike the cue ball so that it hits the cushion and the object ball simultaneously.

Once I played a combination that I thought was a sure thing, rather than going after a ball hanging near the pocket that really *was* a sure thing. I missed the combination and lost the game.

There may be times, such as when you're trying to break up a cluster, that you have no alternative but to try a combination. In that case, pay particular attention to the ball that will be hit right before the one you're trying to pocket. That ball is the key in determining whether you can pocket the one you want to. That ball will tell you whether it's possible to make the shot at a proper angle.

PENALTIES

There are some things to watch for in 14:1. One of them is making sure that when you play safety with an object ball that's frozen against a cushion you either pocket the object ball, make the cue ball contact a cushion after it strikes the object ball, or drive the object ball to another cushion. Otherwise, you lose a point.

Even if you don't violate this rule, you can play safety in this situation only twice in succession. On the third shot, you must either drive the object ball to a different rail or drive the cue ball to any rail after it makes contact with the object ball. Failure to do so will mean that all 15 balls are racked, and you'll have to break as you would at the beginning of the game.

When the cue ball is in contact with an object ball, you may play directly at that object ball, but you must move the object ball and cause the cue ball to strike a cushion or drive that object ball to a cushion. If you don't do one of these, you lose a point.

When you foul and have no points to

which in turn strike the object ball you're trying to pocket. It's another temptation that, for the most part, you ought to resist.

Unless you know that the combination is lined up absolutely straight for the hole, don't shoot for it. In fact, if there's any doubt at all about the combination, go to your alternative shot. And if you have a straight-in shot, by all means take that one first.

your credit, your score becomes minus-1, minus-2, or however many points you owe. When you count, what you owe is deducted from your score.

As mentioned earlier, three scratches in succession cost you a 15-point penalty in addition to one point off for each scratch. To add insult to injury, you then have to break open 15 balls as at the beginning of the game.

A ball that goes into a pocket and bounces out doesn't count as pocketed.

If a cue ball jumps off the table, it counts as a foul, with loss of point and turn. If an object ball goes off the table, it just ends the inning. The ball is spotted.

If the cue ball jumps up accidentally as a result of a legal stroke, or deliberately, by the player's elevating the butt end of the cue and striking the ball in the center or above center, it's a legal jump. But if you dig under the cue ball with the tip, causing the ball to jump, you lose a point.

SIX BALLS IN SIX POCKETS. Here's how to do one of my favorite trick shots. Balls A and B, the middle balls in each group of three, should be close enough together so that the cue ball can't go through. They should be placed halfway between the side pocket and the diamond, in the center of the table. The end balls should be touching A and B, but be placed at angles toward the corner pockets. Hit the cue ball below center, using a hard stroke.

chapter 4
THE GAMES PEOPLE PLAY

There are innumerable games other than 14:1 that you can play on a pool table, all of them fun and all of them requiring combinations of the skills and strategies dealt with in previous chapters.

On the following pages are several —but by no means all—of the popular games that players have found exciting and challenging over the years. There's nothing to prevent you from taking elements of some of them and combining them into original games of your own. Please note: many of the games are played with variations of the rules given here.

There should be enough games here to keep you happy at the billiards table for a long time. For all of the rules and specifics, see the official rule book of the Billiard Congress of America.

BASIC POCKET BILLIARDS

Object

The game of *basic pocket billiards* involves only one rack of balls, and the first player or team to pocket eight balls wins the game.

The Break

In basic pocket billiards, players lag, choose, or draw lots for the opening break. The break is done with cue ball in hand. The player who breaks must either pocket a ball or drive two object balls in addition to the cue ball to a cushion. If your opponent breaks and fails to do this, you get cue ball in hand. You can place the cue ball anywhere within the head string.

In match or tournament play, the starting player must either pocket a ball or drive two object balls to a cushion. If he fails, his opponent has the option of accepting the balls in position or insisting on a reracking until the opening player complies.

Rules

In most respects, basic pocket billiards

is played like 14:1, but there are some differences. After the opening shot, you have to call the ball or balls you intend to pocket, but you don't have to designate the pocket at which you're aiming. On the opening shot, you get credit for any balls pocketed; you don't have to call them.

Later, if you call more than one ball, you have to pocket all the balls you called, or none will count. If you miss a called ball, but the cue ball touches any object ball, it's not an error. Like 14.1, basic pocket billiards involves continuous play.

Penalties

In basic pocket billiards penalties consist of forfeiting one ball and point, plus any balls pocketed on the foul stroke.

A player loses a point each time he or she fails to comply with break shot requirements. Other grounds for penalties include scratching the cue ball in a pocket; forcing the cue ball off the table; shooting while the balls are in motion; striking the cue ball twice on the same stroke; touching a ball with the cue in any way except on a legal stroke; or failing, after the opening stroke, to pocket a ball, cause an object ball to hit a cushion, or cause the cue ball to hit a cushion after striking the object ball.

Playing Strategy/Winning Tips

Because only eight wins this game, it's important to avoid scratching and imperative that you don't leave your opponent an easy shot that can start him on a winning run.

FIFTEEN-BALL POCKET BILLIARDS

Object

The object of this game, which is played with a cue ball and 15 object balls, is to be the first to score 61 points. The numbers on the object balls total 120 points, and you get the number of points on the ball that you pocket. For example, the 7-ball is worth 7 points.

The Break

The balls are racked up in a triangle, with the 15-ball at the foot spot. The next high-numbered balls are placed near the 15-ball. On the opening break, you must either pocket a ball or drive at least two object balls to a cushion. You don't have to call your shots, either on the break or on subsequent play. If you fail to break properly, your opponent has the option of requiring you to break again.

Rules

After the opening stroke of the game, if you don't pocket a ball you must either drive an object ball to a cushion or make the cue ball hit a cushion after making contact with an object ball.

All balls made on one legal stroke are credited to the player who pockets them.

If the game ends in a tie, you can either play the whole game over or spot the 15-ball on the foot spot, lag for the next shot, and reopen play with the cue ball in hand. Whoever scores the 15-ball wins.

Penalties

Penalties are costly in this game. You lose *three* points each time you fail to comply with the requirements of the opening break shot. You also lose three points if the cue ball is pocketed; if a ball is not pocketed and you fail either to drive an object ball to a cushion or make the cue ball go into a rail after it hits an object ball; if you hit the cue ball off the table; if you shoot out of turn; if you hit a ball when it's in motion; and if you fail to have one foot on the floor when you're stroking. If you commit

THE BALLS AS THEY ARE RACKED FOR ROTATION.

more than one foul simultaneously, you lose only three points.

Playing Strategy/Winning Tips

It obviously pays in this game to go after the high-numbered balls. But a word of caution: don't take a nearly impossible shot at, say, the 14-ball and run the risk of ending your inning when you've got a safer shot at a 6-ball or 7-ball. Take the shots you can make.

ROTATION

Object

One of the old standbys of the pool table is *rotation*, which is also called *sixty-one* because scoring 61 points clinches the game. You get points according to the number on the ball you pocket—one point for the 1-ball, two points for the 2-ball, and so on. The game is like fifteen-ball pocket billiards, with one major exception: in rotation, after the opening break, you have to pocket the balls in rotation, starting with the 1-ball and working on up.

The Break

The balls are racked up with the 1-ball in front and the 2-ball and 3-ball in the left and right rear corners of the triangle, respectively. The rest of the balls are racked at random.

Players lag, choose, or draw lots for the break. If you're the one who breaks, you must make the 1-ball your first object ball. If you fail to contact the 1-ball first on the break shot, your inning ends. Any other balls pocketed on the shot are spotted. Your opponent accepts the ball in position and makes the 1-ball his first object.

If you do make contact with the 1-ball on the break you get credit for any other balls that are pocketed. So on the break, while aiming at the 1-ball, try to break all the balls wide open.

Rules

After the 1-ball is pocketed, the 2-ball becomes the legal object ball, then the 3-ball, and so forth. The lowest-numbered ball on the table is always the object ball. The cue ball must strike the legal object ball before making contact with any other ball, or your inning ends. As long as you first make contact with the legal object ball, you're entitled to all balls pocketed on the shot, whether or not you pocket the legal object ball.

By the way, there is no scratch in rotation. If the cue ball should go in the pocket, there is no point penalty. But it is then the end of your inning.

Balls illegally pocketed are spotted on the *long string*, an imaginary line that runs from the foot spot to the center of the foot rail (Diagram 15). Balls are spotted in numerical order. For example, if the 1-ball and 3-ball are illegally pocketed, the 1-ball is placed on the foot spot and the 3-ball is frozen right behind it on the string. If the foot spot is occupied, the spotted balls are placed as close as possible to the spot, in numerical order. Never move the cue ball or an object ball that happens to be on the long string to make room for a ball to be spotted. Instead, place the spotted balls either in front or behind those object balls on the long string. If the cue ball is on the long string so that it interferes with spotting of an object ball, the object ball is placed in front or behind the cue ball and as close to it as possible.

If the entire long string is occupied, the balls to be spotted are placed in front

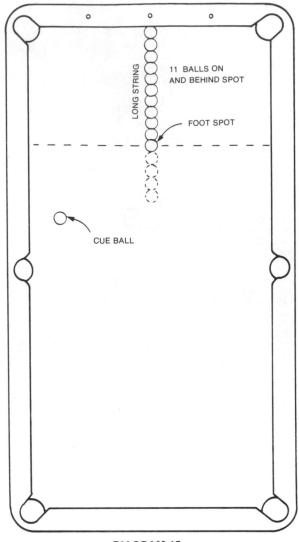

DIAGRAM 15.
Spotting balls.

of the foot spot and as close to it as possible.

If an object ball jumps the table, it is spotted. If you cause one or more object balls to jump the table but you made contact with the legal object ball first, you are credited with any object balls you pocketed on the stroke. If you fail to score, your inning ends.

If the cue ball jumps the table, it's an error and ends your inning. Any balls pocketed on that stroke are spotted, and your opponent continues with cue ball in hand.

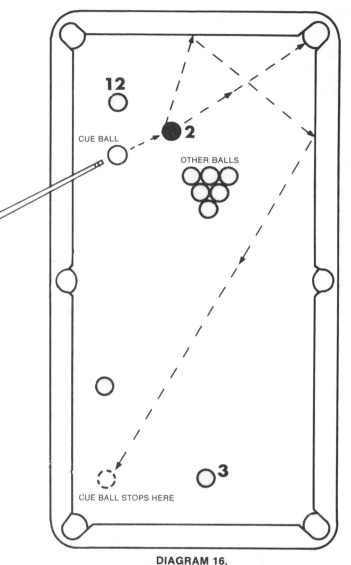

DIAGRAM 16.
The 12-ball is an easy shot, but the game of rotation requires that the 3-ball be made after the 2-ball, a very difficult shot. I would use a hard follow with right-hand English to pocket the 2-ball and get into position for the 3-ball.

If the legal object ball lies between the head string and the head of the table, and you've got cue ball in hand, the legal object ball is placed on the foot spot.

Playing Strategy/Winning Tips

The rules of rotation prescribe the strategy you must employ. You've got to make sure that you hit the legal object ball first. This is a game where you may be forced into a carom shot because

your object ball may be hidden by other balls. If this happens, proceed with the utmost care and caution. Diagram 16 shows how I would handle a typical playing situation.

LINE-UP POCKET BILLIARDS

Object

The object of *line-up pocket billiards* is to score a predetermined number of points before your opponent does. You get one point for each ball you legally pocket. You have to call the ball you intend to pocket as well as the pocket at which you're aiming. If other balls go in along with the one you called, you get credit for each of them as well.

You and your opponent decide on what score wins—25-, 50-, and 100-point games are typical.

The Break

If you open the game, you must either pocket a *called* ball or drive two object balls to a cushion. If you fail to do one or the other, you lose *two* points, and your opponent can make you break again and keep breaking until you comply with the requirements. You lose two points for each successive failure.

Rules

All balls pocketed are spotted on the long string line, the imaginary line from the foot spot to the center of the foot rail. If you should score all 15 balls, they're spotted on the string line. You continue to play, shooting the cue ball from where it came to rest after your last stroke.

After the opening break, any foul costs a point. Balls scored on a foul don't count, and if you have no points at the

THE BALLS AS THEY ARE RACKED FOR EIGHT BALL.

time you foul, you owe a point, which is deducted after you score.

After a legal break shot on which the starting player hasn't scored, the opponent accepts the balls in position and must call the shots—ball and pocket—on all his or her strokes. A player continues until he or she misses, then records the points and spots the balls he or she has scored. Balls are spotted as in the game of rotation.

Generally, the same rules apply in lineup pocket billiards as in 14:1. Balls scored on foul strokes don't count, and penalties—one point for each foul, but only one point if the player fouls more than once on the same stroke—are deducted from the player's score.

Playing Strategy/Winning Tips

Play position as much as possible.

EIGHT BALL

You've heard the expression, "behind the eight ball." This is the game it comes from. In *eight ball*, you must try as hard not to do anything to lose the game as you try to do things to win it.

Object

The object of *eight ball* is to pocket a specific seven of the 15 object balls and *then* pocket the 8-ball before your opponent sinks his or her seven object balls and the 8-ball.

One player or side has to pocket the balls numbered 1 to 7; the other, the balls from 9 to 15. The 8-ball must be saved for last.

The game is played with a cue ball and 15 object balls, which are racked at the foot spot, with the 8-ball in the center of the triangle.

The Break

If you break, you don't have to call any shots. If you pocket one or more balls on the break, you have your choice of making the 1-7 balls or the 9-15 group your objects. If you don't pocket a ball on the break, your opponent gets the choice, and you take the other category.

Rules

The player gets credit for all balls legally pocketed—except balls that are in the opponent's group. If you pocket a ball belonging to your competitor, he or she gets credit for it. If you pocket only one of your opponent's balls and none of your own, it's a miss and your turn ends.

After all the balls in your group have been pocketed, you may go after the 8-ball. Although you didn't have to call the other shots, you must call this one.

If you're shooting directly at the 8-ball without banking, you must either pocket the ball or make it or the cue ball contact a cushion after striking the 8-ball. If you fail to do either of these, you *lose the game*!

If you pocket the 8-ball on the opening break, you lose the game. If you accidentally pocket the 8-ball before you pocket all the balls in your numerical group, you lose the game. If you're banking the 8-ball, you must hit the 8-ball or you lose the game.

When you're playing for the 8-ball, you must hit that ball first. If you pocket it on a combination, you lose the game.

Remember, you've got to call the pocket where you intend to drop the 8-ball. If it goes into a pocket you didn't designate, you lose the game.

When you're shooting to make the 8-ball, you lose the game if the cue ball scratches in a pocket.

Spotting

When you have cue ball in hand and there are object balls within the head string, place the object ball that's nearest to the string on the foot spot. You do the same thing when the 8-ball is the object ball and is lying within the head string and you've got the cue ball in hand.

Special Requirements

Rules may vary widely in eight ball—and you and your opponent can alter them to suit yourselves. If you want to make the game harder, here are some of the official requirements.

If your group of balls is the low-numbered one, you must pocket the 1-ball in the right side pocket as you face the foot of the table. If you've got the high-numbered balls, you must put the 15-ball in the left side pocket. If these balls aren't dropped into those designated pockets, they're spotted and respotted until they are.

Combination shots are permissible at any time except when you're trying to pocket the 8-ball.

Playing Strategy/Winning Tips

Try to make your set of balls without breaking up clusters or any types of trouble balls that might be of advantage to your opponent.

Among veteran players, games played at a pool table are divided into categories—"money games," "gentlemen's games," and "girl friend games."

The two games preferred for wagering are *nine ball* and *one pocket*. The reason these are the favorites of money players is that they're finished quickly, and hustlers like to win or lose their

THE BALLS AS THEY ARE RACKED FOR NINE BALL.

money fast. You can enjoy playing these two games whether or not you gamble on them.

NINE BALL

Object

In pool, the biggest money game by far is *nine ball*, whose object, as you can tell from the name, is to sink the 9-ball.

The Break

For this game the balls are racked up in the triangle with the 1-ball at the head and the 9-ball in the middle. The other balls are placed at random.

Rules

The strategy in nine ball is to break the balls wide open and try to sink any one of them. Then, beginning with the 1-ball, you try to sink the balls in numerical order until you sink the 9-ball. You can play a combination involving the 9-ball, just as long as you also hit the ball you're aiming at. If you should hit the 1-ball and that hits the 9-ball and they both go in, you win. You need a good bit of luck. You don't have to call your shots.

Playing Strategy/Winning Tips

This is one game in which it's advantageous to break, because you might make a ball and continue until you run out. You might even make the 9-ball on the break. When I break in nine ball, I place the cue ball almost in the center of the table, just 2 or 3 inches off the head spot, and aim for the center of the cue ball, driving it right at the middle of the 1-ball. I hit it as hard as I can and hope.

The one thing you have to be careful of is scratching, even though it won't cost you a point. You can't let your cue ball go into a pocket or your turn ends and your opponent will probably run out.

ONE-POCKET

Object

In *one pocket*, you and your opponent each select a pocket as your own before the game begins. Most likely, you'll pick one of the pockets at the foot of the table, since that's where balls are likely to go on the break. The object of the game is to sink eight balls in your pocket. The first player to do so wins the game.

Rules

Balls do not have to be played in rotation or any specific order, and you don't have to call the balls you're trying to sink. Just make eight of them in your pocket.

Playing Strategy/Winning Tips

This is a game where defensive play is critical and the mental aspect is strong. It's like a chess game in that you're thinking four or five moves ahead and, even as you're moving offensively, you're playing defense. Try to leave your opponent the hardest bank possible. Don't take gambles, because in the long run you'll lose out.

Let's say we lag and I break. Since you seldom are able to make a ball in your pocket on the break, I would hit what's called a *safe break*—a very easy hit to protect myself. I'll try to get as many balls as possible near my pocket, without leaving you a clear shot at yours. If I'm successful, it puts you on the defensive. You have to get the balls that are near my pocket out of there because, if you don't, I'll probably sink two or three or more. So you have to protect yourself at all times. If you make a tactical mistake, you'll have to be very lucky to get away with it.

Carom or bank shots are an important part of this game since, if your opponent is skillful, you're not going to be left with any straight-on shots. But caroms take a lot of skill and I don't recommend them until your game is well developed.

POKER POCKET BILLIARDS

If you like playing cards as well as pool, *poker pocket billiards* is a fun game to try. It's played with a white cue ball and a special set of 16 object balls. Four of the object balls have a "J" on them. The

"J" stands for jack, as in poker played with cards. Four other balls are marked with "Q" for queen; four more with "K" for king, and the remaining four with "A" for ace.

Object: Poker Hand

The object of the game is to get a better poker hand than your opponent. Four of a kind—four aces or four queens, for instance—is the best hand you can get. (Four aces would beat four kings, and so on.) The next best hand is a full house—two of one and three of another, such as a pair of jacks and three kings. Next in order is three of a kind, then two pairs, then a straight (ace, king, queen, jack), and finally, a pair. Poker players will note that the order of best hands is different from the order in the card game of poker.

The Break

The object balls are racked in any order on the foot spot in a diamond shape. One ball is placed up front, then two, then three, then four, three, two, and one. You can flip a coin or lag to decide the break. The player who breaks gets credit for the balls pocketed on the break, providing he or she hasn't fouled.

Rules

No player can pocket more than five balls in a single turn or inning. Any ball you've pocketed legally stays off the table. If one of the opponents is much better than the other, you can equalize the game by allowing each player only one shot at a time.

You foul by failing to hit an object ball, pocketing the cue ball, driving the cue ball off the table, failing to keep at least one foot on the floor while stroking, or touching the cue ball with anything but the cue tip. It's also a foul if you touch any object ball except on legal contact by the cue ball.

There will be times in this game that you'll want to miss deliberately rather than pocket a ball that won't improve your hand. You can do this, but you must either drive an object ball to a cushion or have the cue ball hit a cushion after striking the object ball. Failure to do this is a foul.

The game ends when all balls have been legally pocketed.

When it's your turn, you can try to improve your "hand" if you already have five balls to your credit. If you choose to do so, you continue to shoot in turn, trying to improve your hand by pocketing the ball that would go best with it.

You can, if you and your opponent agree ahead of time, decide to make one ball wild. If you should decide, say, that the J ball is wild, you can consider a J ball that you pocket as any card you want.

GOLF POCKET BILLIARDS

Another game that borrows from a different pastime is *golf pocket billiards*.

Object

The object of this game is to play six holes in the fewest possible strokes.

The Break

You use only a white cue ball and any one object ball. To start, place the cue ball on the center spot and the object ball on the foot spot. If you're the starting player, you have to bank the object ball against the foot cushion on the first stroke, as you attempt to pocket the ball in the left side pocket.

Rules

If you miss the bank shot on the first

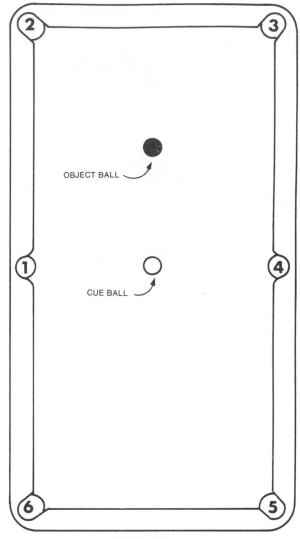

DIAGRAM 17.
The balls set up for golf pocket billiards.

stroke, you *continue* to shoot until you pocket the ball, shooting either directly at the object ball or banking it, as you see fit. After that first stroke, you're not compelled to bank. When you finally pocket the ball in the left side pocket, you add up the strokes it took you and keep that as your score for the first hole.

Now it's your opponent's turn. Again the balls are spotted—the cue ball on the center spot and the object ball on the foot spot. Your opponent, too, must bank to the lower rail on the first stroke, as he or she tries to pocket the ball in the left side pocket. Your opponent's score for the first hole is totalled.

It's your turn again. The object ball is spotted on the foot spot once more, but the cue ball is left where it was when your opponent scored his or her opening shot. This time, you're aiming to pocket the ball in the *upper* left corner hole. You don't have to bank this shot, although you can. Keep stroking until you sink the ball.

The object ball is spotted once more, the cue ball left where it was when you pocketed the ball, and your opponent now tries to make the ball in the upper left corner hole in as few shots as possible.

After that keep alternating as you aim for the upper righthand corner pocket, then the righthand side pocket, the right-hand lower corner pocket, and, finally, the lefthand lower corner pocket—*in that order*. Each player has an inning at each hole. The one who completes the six holes in the fewest number of strokes wins the game.

Partners

If you should play the game with partners, as many players like to do, the partners' scores are added together, and the team with the lowest number of strokes wins.

In partners, if you take the opening stroke and miss, your partner then attempts to pocket the ball, and you keep alternating until the ball is dropped into the designated hole. If you should make the ball on the first shot, your partner will lead off the next inning.

On a change of turn, the only time the object ball is not spotted is when the object ball lies within the head string.

Penalties

Scratches occur in golf pocket billiards when you pocket the cue ball or when you sink the object ball in the wrong pocket. The penalty adds *three* strokes to your score, plus the one stroke for the shot. If you should double-scratch—pocket the object ball in the wrong hole and also pocket the cue ball—you're assessed only one penalty. The scratched balls are spotted and you continue playing. This is different from most other pocket billiard games, where you lose your turn when you fail to pocket a ball.

On every shot the object ball either has to be pocketed or hit a cushion or the cue ball has to hit a cushion after it strikes the object ball. If you fail to do any of these things, it will cost you three extra strokes in addition to one for your shot. Play continues with the balls left where they are.

BASEBALL POCKET BILLIARDS

Object

The winner in *baseball pocket billiards* is the player who has the most runs after nine innings of play.

The Break

Baseball pocket billiards is played with 21 object balls numbered from 1 through 21, as well as a white cue ball. Rack up the object balls in a 21-ball triangle, with the 1-ball on the foot spot (called *home plate* in this game); the 2-ball at the left corner, and the 3-ball at the right corner. The 9-ball (called the *pitcher*), is placed somewhere near the center of the rack.

Rules

Every player has nine innings at the table,

which he or she plays in succession. In other words, your inning continues until you miss or end your turn as the result of a foul, and you keep going until you've completed nine innings.

The runs you score correspond to the numbers on the balls you pocket. (The 16-ball, for instance, is worth 16 runs.) You can lag, draw lots, or flip a coin to start, but it really doesn't matter, since you and your opponent will have an equal chance to score.

On the break shot, you get credit for all the balls you pocket. After that, you must call your shots—which ball you're planning to put in which pocket. If you pocket other balls in addition to the ball you've called, you get credit for them as well. If others go in, but not the one you've called, it's a scoreless inning. If you should pocket all 21 balls before you've had nine innings, the balls are reracked and you keep going until you've completed nine innings.

Any number of players can play baseball pocket billiards, but before the game is over everyone has to have had nine innings at the table.

If you scratch, it completes your inning and you get 0 runs. You then play your next inning. If you make a scratch without pocketing an object ball, you still have a scoreless inning. The penalty for a scratch is forfeit of all the balls pocketed on your foul stroke, plus the last called ball that you legally pocketed. If you had no balls to your credit at the time you scratched, you spot the next called ball that you score.

If you pocket a ball and make a scratch, you spot the object ball on ''home plate''—the foot spot, or if that is occupied, immediately behind it.

It helps to post each player's score, inning by inning, on a scoresheet.

BOY MEETS GIRL

Object

A game with a double standard is *boy meets girl* or *Mr. & Mrs. pocket billiards*. The object of the game is to score 61 points first, but the rules are stricter for some players than for others.

The Break

The game is played with 15 object balls, numbered from 1 through 15, and the white cue ball. Object balls are racked at the foot spot, with the 1-ball at the apex of the triangle and the 2-ball and 3-ball at the left and right rear corners, respectively.

If you're going to break, the 1-ball has to be your first object ball, whether you're male or female, and you get credit for any balls pocketed on that first shot if your cue ball made contact with the 1-ball first.

Rules

The game is based on the old-fashioned idea that one sex is weaker than the other. The requirements of play are tougher for one player than for the other. Actually, the game is ideal for equalizing any two players whose pocket billiards skills vary greatly.

For purposes of discussion only, let's say the woman is the weaker player in pocket billiards. In this game, therefore, the woman is exempt from pocketing balls in rotation. She doesn't have to call her shots, and she gets credit for all balls pocketed on kiss shots or combinations. The man, meanwhile, must pocket the balls in rotation (the 1-ball first, the 2-ball second, and so on). He must have hit the numerical object ball first to get credit for other object balls pocketed on kiss shots or combinations. If the man pockets an object ball without having hit the numerical object ball first, it ends his inning and the pocketed ball or balls on that stroke are spotted.

After the break shot, the man must make the balls in numerical order, while the women do not. Players get points corresponding to the numbers of the balls they pocketed. (A 6-ball is worth six points, and so on.)

Usually men are better players, but that's not always the case. Jimmy Caras's daughter used to embarrass boys she'd bring home on dates by beating them at the pool table. But that's exceptional and that's why boy meets girl, which makes it easier for weaker players to score, is such a good equalizer. Obviously, a woman should play by the male rules, and vice versa, if she is the better player.

Penalties

If the cue ball is scratched in a pocket and no object balls are pocketed, you lose your turn but there's no penalty. Your competitor has the cue ball in hand. If the other player is the man and his legal numerical object ball is within the head string, the legal object ball is spotted and he plays with cue ball in hand. If the incoming player is a woman, she has cue ball in hand and may shoot at any object ball of her choice.

If any player scratches the cue ball in a pocket, the object balls pocketed on that stroke are spotted. If a man pockets an object ball without having first hit the numerical object ball, the pocketed ball or balls on that stroke are spotted.

Balls are spotted in numerical order, from the foot spot back toward the foot cushion, as in rotation.

CRIBBAGE POCKET BILLIARDS

Object

The object of *cribbage pocket billiards*

is to score more cribbages than your opponent. To score a cribbage—or one point—you've got to pocket two balls whose point value totals 15 (say the 6-ball and 9-ball, or the 3-ball and 12-ball) in the same inning. The 15-ball counts as a cribbage in itself, but that must be left for last.

The Break

This game is played with the cue ball and 15 numbered balls. You start cribbage pocket billiards in the same way as you do 14:1, with the balls racked in a triangle at the foot spot in no particular numerical order.

If you open, you don't have to call your break shot, but, as in 14:1, you've got to drive two or more object balls as well as the cue ball to a cushion or pocket an object ball. If you fail to comply with these regulations, you lose a point and you can be compelled to break again. If you miss the second time, your opponent accepts the balls in position.

Rules

It doesn't count to pocket more than two balls that add up to 15 (say the 4-ball, 5-ball, and 6-ball). That would be an error and end your inning.

The 15-ball must be left for last. If you score a cribbage legally (two balls totalling 15 in the same inning), your turn continues, and you can try for another in the same inning. If you should make, say, the 3-ball, but miss the 12-ball, the 3-ball is spotted.

Whoever has the most cribbages when all balls are pocketed wins the game.

Playing Strategy/Winning Tips

If you don't have relatively easy shots at one or both of the balls you need for a particular cribbage, play for safety.

FORTY-ONE POCKET BILLIARDS

Object

This is a game in which an *exact* score is necessary to win. Your aim is to score 41 points, which is a combination of the point value of the balls you pocket plus a private number that you're given. You must keep the number from your opponents until you're ready to declare that you've got 41.

The Break

The game is played with a cue ball and 15 object balls, plus a leather shake bottle containing small balls or "peas," which are usually numbered from 1 to 15. Rotation of play is determined by throwing each player a small ball from the bottle. The player with the lowest number has to break. Before play starts, each player is thrown another numbered ball from the bottle—his private number.

Rules

Once you've pocketed the number of points that, when added to your private number, totals 41, you announce and show your private number.

One rule that's very different about this game is that, whether or not you pocket any balls, you're allowed just one shot per inning. If you should pocket more than one ball on a single stroke in an inning, you get credit for them all.

If all the balls should be pocketed before anyone has 41, the player whose count is closest to 41 wins. If you play safety, you have to make the cue ball hit a cushion before or after contacting an object ball. Otherwise, you scratch and owe a ball.

Bursting

If you should get more than 41 points,

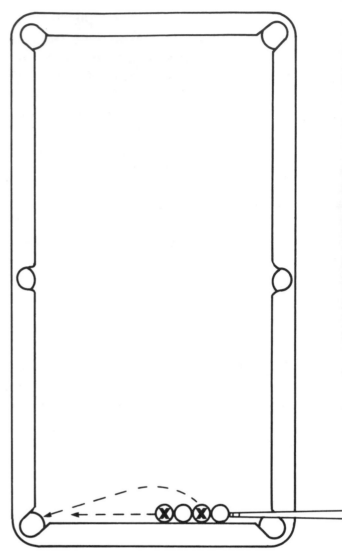

DIAGRAM 18.
Trick shot—the two in a hole shot. Three object balls are frozen to the rail. *Push* the cue ball on the right side (right-hand English). The two outer balls will go in the pocket and the center ball will not.

that's a *burst* and you must declare it or be disqualified from continuing in the game. If you want, you can get a new private number and begin again.

Penalties

If you miss or pocket the cue ball, you've scratched, and you owe a ball to the table, plus balls you may have scored on the shot. If you have more than one ball to your credit, you can spot any ball you choose. If you owe a ball and you've got none in your rack, you have to spot the first ball you legally count. If you score more than one, when you owe one to the table, again you may choose which one to spot.

When you burst and all your balls are spotted, the last ball pocketed has to be placed on the foot spot or as near as possible behind it.

BOTTLE POCKET BILLIARDS

Bottle pocket billiards is another game that requires an exact score to win. It also makes use of a shake bottle.

Object

Any number can play the game, and the player who first scores exactly 31 points wins. If you should score more than 31, though, it counts as a miss. Your inning ends and your score becomes the difference between 31 and your total. Suppose you've scored 37. Your score would become 6, the difference between 31 and 37.

The Break

A cue ball and two object balls, numbered 1 and 2, are used in the game. At the start of the game, the 1-ball is placed at the foot cushion in front of the left diamond on the foot rail. The 2-ball is placed against the foot cushion at the right diamond on the foot rail. The shake bottle is placed open end down on the center spot.

Rules

When you score exactly 31, you've got to announce your total before your opponent takes his or her turn at the table. If you fail to do this, you can't announce

until your next regular turn. If an opponent should score 31 and announces it before your next turn, he or she is the winner.

Scoring

Points are scored in different ways. A carom on the two object balls counts 1 point. Pocketing the 1-ball counts 1 point. Pocketing the 2-ball counts 2 points. A carom from the ball that upsets the shake bottle counts 5 points.

It's possible to score 9 points on the same shot, combining all these feats.

Should a carom from an object ball stand the shake bottle on its base, you automatically win the game for this miraculous accomplishment.

If you start the game, you don't have to call your shot but you do have to make either the 1- or 2-ball your first object. And on all shots that follow, a ball has to be the first object. The bottle never becomes the direct object of the cue ball until the cue ball has contacted an object ball. If an object ball hits the bottle before the cue ball makes contact with that object ball, the shot doesn't count.

Whenever the bottle is upset, it must be placed with its open end down as close as possible to where the open end of it lay when it came to rest after being upset.

When the bottle is forced off the table or into a pocket, the player loses his turn and the bottle is spotted on the center spot. If an object ball forces the bottle to a cushion, into a pocket, or off the table, you lose your turn.

Fouls

Anytime you foul your inning ends, the points you scored on the stroke don't count, and you lose one point. You commit a foul if you fail to hit an object ball on a stroke; if an object ball, your hand, clothing, or cue stick upsets the bottle; if the cue ball is forced off the table or pocketed; if the cue ball upsets the bottle before hitting the object ball; or if you shoot without at least one foot touching the floor.

ONE-AND-NINE BALL

Object

One-and-nine ball is a four-handed game, with the partners selected after the game has started. The team that scores 61 points first wins the game. Balls are valued according to their face numbers.

The Break

Balls are racked as in the game of rotation, with the 1-ball on the foot spot at the apex of the triangle and the 2-ball and 3-ball in the left and right rear corners, respectively.

Rules

Played with a white cue ball and 15 numbered object balls, the game uses the rules of 14:1 and rotation pocket billiards.

The balls must be pocketed in rotation. The player who scores the 1-ball automatically becomes the partner of the player who pockets the 9-ball. If it turns out that the same player pockets both the 1- and 9-balls, he or she becomes partner of the player who scores the 10-ball. If the 10-ball is off the table, the one who pockets the 11-ball is his or her partner.

It's possible that each side may have 60 points when all the balls are pocketed. If so, the player who pocketed the last ball places that ball on the foot spot and has the cue ball in hand within the head string. He continues his inning. Play con-

tinues until one side or the other pockets the lone ball on the table.

COWBOY POCKET BILLIARDS

Object

Cowboy pocket billiards combines carom and pocket billiards. The object of the game is to score 101 points first, but points are scored in different ways at different stages of the game.

The game is played with a white cue ball and three object balls numbered 1, 3, and 5. Each object ball has a point value equal to its number.

The Break

To start the game, the 3-ball is placed on the foot spot, the 5-ball on the center spot, and the 1-ball on the head spot. The starting player has cue ball in hand, which, as you remember, means that he or she can place it anywhere within the head string. The 3-ball is the first object ball.

Rules

The winning score is 101 points, with scoring done in stages. The first 90 points are scored this way: Carom on two object balls scores 1 point. Carom on three object balls scores 2 points. Pocketing one or more object balls brings points according to the number on the ball.

After you've scored exactly 90 points, you must make the next ten points by caroms only. When you've scored 100 points, you must score the 101st, the game-winning point, by caroming the cue ball off the 1-ball into a pocket you call or designate without hitting a second object ball. If the cue ball should drop into a pocket that you didn't call, you lose your turn and the points you made in that inning. You would also lose all the points in an inning if you commit a foul.

When an object ball is pocketed, it has to be replaced on its original spot. If the spots are occupied, the pocketed balls are *held out*—kept off the table—until the spots become unoccupied.

However, if the 1-ball is pocketed when you're playing and you've got exactly 100 points, you can have the balls spotted as in the opening of the game and play the cue ball from hand.

If you've got 90 points, you would lose your turn and points scored in an inning if you pocketed an object ball while scoring from 91 to 100.

Except for the prescribed way to score the 101st point, you'd lose your inning and points scored in that turn if you pocket the cue ball. Loss of turn and points scored in that inning also result from forcing the cue ball off the table.

You *forfeit* the game if you pocket the cue ball twice in succession without touching an object ball either time.

If you've got 100 points, you lose your turn and all points made in the same inning if you fail to hit the 1-ball when trying to make the 101st point.

When the cue ball is frozen to an object ball, you must shoot in such a way that you move the object ball and drive the cue ball into a cushion. If you fail to do this, it's a scratch, and you lose your turn and the point made in the inning.

After a cue ball scratch, the incoming player has cue ball in hand. He or she must put it in play behind the head string line and drive it to an object ball or a cushion outside the head string.

SNOOKER

Snooker is played on a 5-by-10-foot table (or 6-by-12-foot) with smaller, rounder pockets than those on a pocket billiards table and with a thinner cue stick than the one used in straight pool.

The game involves 15 red balls, which aren't numbered, and six different-colored balls numbered 2 through 7. The balls are smaller than those used in straight pool.

Object

The object of snooker is to have the highest number of points—when all the balls are off the table.

The Break

The 15 red balls are racked as are balls in regular pocket billiards. The pink ball touches the apex ball on the center line of the table.

On the opening stroke, you have cue ball in hand, but in snooker that means you can put it in play only within a radius of 9⅜ inches or 11½ inches (depending on table size) behind the green, brown and yellow balls, with brown in the center.

To start the game, place the blue ball on the center spot. The black ball goes on a billiard spot near the foot (10½ inches in from the foot rail on a 5-by-10-foot table; 12½ inches in on a 6-by-12-foot table.) The green, brown, and yellow balls are spaced across a balk line parallel to the head rail (23½ inches in on a 5-by-10-foot table, and 29 inches in on a 6-by-12).

You have to contact a red ball first on your opening break shot. Any red balls scored on that opening stroke are to your credit.

Rules

In snooker you must sink any red ball first. (Red balls have a one-point value.)

Then you may sink any numbered ball, for which you get a point value equal to the number of that ball. When a numbered ball is pocketed, you respot it on the foot spot. A red ball is left in the pocket. You keep alternating—red ball, numbered ball—until all the red balls have been made. Then the numbered balls have to be pocketed in rotation, again with the points awarded according to the number on the ball. When all the numbered balls have been sunk, the player with the highest point total is the winner. You don't have to call the red balls, but you must announce the numbered ball you're aiming to make. You don't have to call the pocket.

The object balls and their point value are as follows: yellow, 2; green, 3; brown, 4; blue, 5; pink, 6, and black, 7.

Red balls are never spotted, even if they're illegally pocketed or driven off the table. Numbered balls scored are spotted on their original spots, unless the appropriate spot is occupied, in which case the last pocketed ball is placed on the next lowest spot. The black ball, for instance, if its space were occupied, would be placed where the pink ball is usually spotted. When all the red balls are off the table, the pocketed numbered balls stay in the pockets after being legally scored. Improper spotting results in a foul, unless your opponent fails to detect it. The foul has to be announced before the next stroke.

Two balls, other than two reds, can't be pocketed on the same stroke. Two balls, other than two reds, must not be struck simultaneously. You can't score if you pocket a red ball legally and pocket a numbered ball on the same stroke.

Getting Snookered

You're said to be *snookered* when you

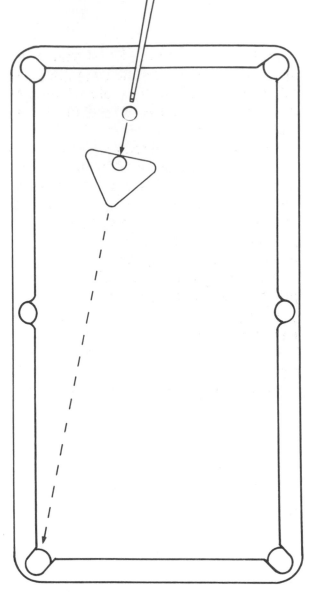

DIAGRAM 19.
Another trick shot. Hit the cue ball hard, above center, with the butt of the cue stick elevated. The cue ball will jump into the triangle, hit the object ball, and force it to jump out and go into the pocket.

can't shoot in a straight line at a ball because of the way other balls are located on the table.

When you're snookered, you still must strike the ball or balls you're on first, even if it means banking the shot.

If, say, you're snookered on reds, and you hit one of the numbered balls first, you've fouled.

If you're on a numbered ball when you're snookered, you must call or nominate the numbered ball you're on and strike that one first before hitting any other object ball on the table. Failure to do so is a foul; so is failure to hit any ball on the table.

After a foul, the incoming player has the choice of taking or refusing the next shot. If he or she refuses the other player must shoot again. Every time a player continues to foul, a penalty of *seven* points is forfeited and the incoming player still has the option.

All fouls involve the forfeiture of seven points—the points are either *added* to your opponent's score or subtracted from your own.

If you don't try to strike the ball, you forfeit seven points. If you do it again on your next turn, you forfeit another seven, and your opponent has the option of accepting the shot or making you play until you execute a legal shot.

Safety play is legal, but you've got to drive a red ball, or a numbered ball you call, to the cushion, or cause the cue ball to strike a cushion after hitting the ball that is on. You can't pocket a ball and call it a safety.

Playing Strategy/Winning Tips

Because of the shape and size of the pockets, this game is particularly difficult. So, unless your object ball is in an easy position to be made, safety play is a big factor. Even a shot within inches of the pocket can be missed, so be very careful and make every shot count.

TAKE LESSONS FROM AN EXPERT . . . if you're really serious about becoming a good pocket billiards player. After the pro has taught you the basics, the way to develop your skills is to practice, practice, practice—for at least an hour a day.

chapter 5
WHAT MAKES A GOOD PLAYER

Earlier we talked about the equipment you need to play pocket billiards, but we didn't mention the most important factors of all: the physical and mental qualities that ultimately determine how good a player you can be.

To be a player of *championship* calibre, you must either be born with a special talent or else start playing when you're an infant and keep at it throughout your life. But whether or not you have that natural something it takes to be a champion, you can still develop into a very good player, regardless of the age at which you start, your sex, size, build, or strength—provided you have a few things going for you to start with and you're willing to work hard.

Basically, you need three qualities to be a competent pool player: good coordination, good eyesight, and the right mental attitude.

If you're a born klutz, you probably won't ever be champion, but you can develop your coordination to the top limits of your natural ability through practice. Playing the game is the best means.

Eyesight is naturally an important factor in playing pool, simply because you have to see where you're hitting the ball. I happen to be nearsighted and wear glasses, but I don't wear them when I'm playing. Through some kind of happy turn of fate, I can see the length of the table without special lenses. I can hit a ball as *thin* as I want, *breeze* it, or just rock it back and forth, if I want to.

The better your eyesight, the more finely you'll be able to cut a ball. But even if your eyesight is poor, if you wear glasses, you can still learn to play well. Just compensate by concentrating on position play so that you won't have to cut the ball as precisely in order to pocket it. In other words, the easier the angle of the shot you leave yourself, the less squinting and precision-shooting you'll need to make a ball.

Generally speaking, pool is a game of areas—you'll seldom hit the ball to the *exact* point you're aiming at every time. Not even a Ferguson Jenkins always pitches the ball right into the bullseye center of the catcher's glove on every toss. If you can hit the ball to the general area of the pocket, you will, if all goes well, make the shot.

MENTAL ATTITUDE

One of the biggest factors in how well you play pocket billiards is mental attitude. If you don't have the desire to excel, you'll never be more than a fair player, if that. If you don't have the will to win and the ability to play under pressure, you're not going to play well. You certainly can't be considered championship calibre, although even at the top ranks, there are some players who choke when the going gets rough. The ability to play under fire is pretty much an inborn quality—either you have it or you don't—but there are outside factors that can influence you and your mental condition.

If you're pressured by your job or financial burdens, usually you're not going to do well in game competition. You have to be relaxed and well rested, with your mind at ease. When you get out there at the table, your mind must be only on what you're doing. You have to block out everything else—the crowd, your opponent's reputation, the argument you had at home or at work—and concentrate totally on your game. The key word is *concentrate*, whether you're playing for money or for fun, whether you're in a championship match in front of a crowd or relaxing in a friendly game in your own basement.

There will be situations when you've got to be willing to take risks in the game, without getting wild, in order to win. If, for instance, there's a trouble ball that should be pocketed at once, and you don't have the courage to try the shot, it could mean you might as well put up your hands and surrender because your opponent is probably going to start a run that wins the game. If you are willing to take the chance, though, you've got to be cool enough to give yourself the best possible chance of making the ball. Pool is 80 percent skill and 20 percent luck. If you can play under pressure, you've got a much better chance that your luck will be good.

Confidence

A significant part of proper mental conditioning is self-confidence. If you don't have the confidence that you're going to succeed in life, you're probably going to wind up a failure. It's also true of pocket billiards. You've got to believe you can do it. Wanting to is the first step.

Some players try to psych themselves up by bragging a lot, the way Muhammad Ali does, trying to convince themselves they're the best. Sometimes this strategy works, but sometimes it doesn't.

It's good to be confident, but you should guard against *over*confidence. It can cost you points and games. If you think you're much better, you might be tempted to spot an opponent 49 points in a 50-point game, ignoring the simple arithmetic fact that he needs only one point to win. Pocket billiards is an easy game to handicap. You can spot points, games, anything to even up a match. There's no formula as to how much of a handicap you can give. Just base it on how much better one of you is than the other, and don't go crazy. Remember, in any given short game, it's possible for almost anyone to beat anyone else who isn't completely out of his class. So you can't be careless.

Late in 1972, I went to Albany, New York, to play some eight ball with five youngsters, all 12 or 13 years old. I was sure I could beat them with one eye closed and one hand tied behind my back. But I wanted them to get some shots at the table, because I knew that they and the people watching would get a charge out of seeing them perform. Well, the first two boys beat me. I missed a couple of shots against one of them, and he got a good run going to win the game. The other just kept pocketing balls until he ran out.

The moral of this story is: Don't let up. Always play as hard as you can, until the last ball is pocketed. When I think I've got an easy match, or when I'm way ahead, I tend to slacken. The fact is that I play better when I'm behind. Maybe it's peculiar, but those are the times I have more of a competitive edge.

Overconfidence sometimes shows when you start taking too much for granted. You think you can make any shot on the table, and so you go in and shoot wildly. That's a form of overconfidence to avoid. The game looks easy, but it isn't, as you'll be reminded if you don't keep your confidence under control.

Sometimes there's only a thin line between a solid bit of self-confidence and overconfidence. When I was 17, I went to Chicago to play in my first tournament, a televised championship in which all the top players were participating. But they all played so badly that I asked Irving Crane, one of the best, "Is this the way all the good players play?" He answered my superior-sounding comment with,

"Son, after you play your first game, come and see me." Luckily, I played pretty well and he gave me a smile that I interpreted as a compliment.

My question to him, I suppose, was a sign of my confidence, despite my age. It was a confidence increased by how poorly the others had started off. You could call it overconfidence, but remember, I'd been playing exhibitions since I was a child and playing for money since I was 16. So I was used to pressure. There were times I played for five dollars when I had only three dollars in my pocket, and that kind of situation puts extra pressure on a player.

Once I was going back to college in Alabama and I had to borrow $35, which I figured would be just about enough to pay for some food and for tolls and gas from New Jersey, where I live. Suddenly, one of the tires had a blowout. For about a hundred miles, I drove on the spare, which had a plug in it. I didn't want to risk going another 500 or more miles on the spare, so I bought a used tire for $13. This left me with about $12 (since I'd already spent 10), which wasn't enough to get all the way to school. So I looked for the local pool room, where I felt certain I could earn some spending money. I found one and got into a four-handed game of nine ball at $2 a game. I lost the first five games—believe me, I wasn't trying to—and was down to my last $2. If I lost the next game, I'd have had to borrow a dime to call somebody to wire me money. But I won that game and more, and ended up with about $54.

I'm not suggesting you take chances like that. I wouldn't have done it myself if it hadn't been necessary. I mention the story only as an example of the importance of confidence in your abilities. Without it, I never could have done it.

PHYSICAL CONDITION

Mental condition is all-important, but don't overlook your physical condition. You play best when you're in the best of health, so try to avoid illness and get as much rest as possible. Don't expect to play well when you've been drinking, and try to stay clear of smoke-filled rooms that will cause eye irritation.

Whether or not you should eat before a game is an individual matter. Some very good players can't play on an empty stomach; some equally good ones can't play on a full stomach. Irving Crane, three-time world champion, is one player who can't play pocket billiards just after he's eaten. He has to go to his hotel room and lie down for an hour or so, and it usually takes him two or three hours in all to digest his food to a point where he's comfortable playing. Others can play immediately, no matter what or how much they've eaten. I'm an in-betweener. Sometimes I can play right after or soon after I've eaten, but I can't play on an empty stomach because when I'm playing hungry, I start feeling sick. You'll find out soon enough in which category you belong.

Thin players seem to be able to last longer at the table than heavier fellows, since they don't sweat as much. I'm 6 feet, 1 inch tall and weigh 220 pounds, and there have been times when I wished I'd started with fewer pounds. So try to keep your weight down.

Unlike a lot of other sports, billiards can be played, and played well, by physically handicapped persons. I've known crippled people, including a man who lost a leg in combat, who aren't hindered by their handicaps when it comes to playing pool.

DRESS COMFORTABLY

Can you think of any competitive sport where players are required to wear a shirt, tie, and jacket when they play? Championship billiards is the only one I can think of. It doesn't make sense to be hindered, when you're out there to play the best you can, but we are. In the World Championships, we have to wear tuxedos! And in the U.S. Open, held in August in Chicago, we must wear ties and jackets—even if it's 180 degrees.

One time we played under lights for "Wide World of Sports," the ABC-TV series, and the television lights made it hotter than ever. I was completely soaked, from my socks to my knuckles. My jacket looked as if somebody had spilled a bucketful of water on it. It's hard to play your best under conditions like those.

But until you get into the World Championships or the U.S. Open, there's no reason for you to dress in anything but what you find most comfortable. There's no regulation uniform. Loose-fitting clothes are the best, because they don't interfere with the fluid motion of your stroke.

PSYCHING

In a game where fractions of an inch can spell victory or defeat, it helps to have nerves of steel. Some players are easily rattled, and some have calm temperaments. Try your best not to let anything disturb you.

A friend of mine, Arthur Cranfield, gets so nervous when he plays that he constantly jumps and dances around and tries to steer the ball in with his body (*body English*). Once, in his nervousness, he spun around accidentally, hit the referee with his cue stick, and knocked him out.

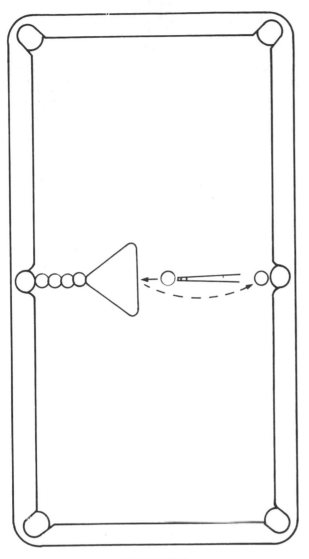

DIAGRAM 20.
Trick shot—The five-ball triangle shot.

One of Arthur's superstitions is to put chalk cubes over all the diamonds along the rails of the table before he shoots. Superstitious habits like these, I suppose, are a form of nervousness.

Some competitors wear special clothing to play. Richard Riggie, a very good player, always wears white socks, no matter what kind of clothing he has on. He even wears them with a tuxedo. He wears the white socks rolled down to his ankles with a rubber band around each sock. It's a habit he's had for years.

Some players talk to themselves. The late Onofrio Lauri used to whistle to himself. There might be 500 spectators watching him, but he'd walk around the table whistling.

Maybe it's because I started playing exhibitions so young, but I'm a player who has the reputation for being able to take almost any distraction in stride.

In the Open in Chicago, there are 1,500 fans watching and four games going on at once. This can be distracting, but usually I enjoy it. I find all the activity takes my mind off what my opponent is doing, and so I don't worry too much.

If somebody at one of the tables makes a great shot just as you're about to shoot, you should have enough savvy to stand up, walk away from the table, and take a drink of water. (You can take a breather anytime you want in a championship match.)

I can't honestly say that crowd noises *never* affect me. When I was 17, I was playing in the Open and needed just one more ball for an upset victory over one of the veteran champions. The crowd was kind of excited and I was pretty jumpy, so I put my cue down and walked around the auditorium with my hands raised, getting everybody to quiet down before I took—and made—the shot.

As cool as I am, I'm constantly rubbing the tip of my cue stick with a dollar bill or sandpaper (which, as I mentioned earlier, *you* shouldn't use anywhere on your shaft). Somehow, it relaxes me and gives me confidence to know that my tip has the right smoothness. Another thing that relaxes me before a match is powdering my hands. You'll find your own little habits that serve to calm you. Don't worry about them, if they do the job.

Several players won't watch TV before a match, and others won't read a newspaper. But that's not superstition. It's just that they don't want to do anything that might be hurting their eyes. A few players like to rest their eyes by keeping them closed for a half hour or so before a match.

Luther Lassiter, the former U.S. Open Champion whom I beat for the title in 1970, was asked recently whether he thought attitude and psyching people out are important in playing pool or billiards. He replied that it might have been at one time, but not nowadays.

Luther, who picked up the nickname Wimpy because of all the hamburgers he ate on the road, was also asked whether he sometimes ate hamburgers during matches to psych out his opponent. "Well that wouldn't be very nice and sporting, now, would it?" he said. "Besides, psyching someone out doesn't really help you win. . ."

Whether or not it helps, some players will resort to all kinds of measures to throw your game off. I had one opponent who went to the bathroom seven times during one rack of balls. It was deliberate, I'm sure, but he wasn't penalized for delaying the game. That's something that's up to the referee's discretion.

The professional referees who oversee professional matches are the sole judges. You can't argue with their decisions and expect to change anything.

Another "sharking" tactic is to casually wave a handkerchief around the eye level of a player, hoping he'll start paying attention to the handkerchief instead of his game.

MONEY-MAKING AND HUSTLING

You can make money out of pool, if you are very good, but not enough to live on. It's probably the poorest-paying professional sport. I think even Chinese-checker players make more. The top championship pays the winner $5,000, and even in expensive Las Vegas tournaments, the promoter makes most of the money, not the competitors.

The only ones who at one time could possibly make a living out of pool were the hustlers, who'd lure unsuspecting lesser players into games for money. Sometimes they'd even lose a few to raise the ante. But, as Luther Lassiter has said, hustling was good 30 years ago, but not now. "Years ago," he commented, "I might find a man who had taken money from everyone he knew for miles around, because he was a good local player and had no competition, and it used to be fun to give him his comeuppance. But nowadays they all know you, thanks to television. So there's no chance of fooling anyone into thinking you're a worse player than you really are."

AMBIDEXTERITY

There are good reasons for you to experiment playing both right-handed *and* left-handed, mainly because conditions will arise on the table where it's difficult to make a shot with your usual power hand.

But don't start fooling with your second hand until you've become pretty good with your first.

I was originally right-handed, but my father, a professional baseball player (and a pretty fair pool player), wanted me to become a left-handed pitcher, and he switched me when I was about four years old. I've been left-handed ever since, but I've always been able to do certain things right-handed. I can play golf with either hand, throw a baseball, bat, or bowl with either hand. And I can play pool with either hand. I'm more proficient left-handed, so in a tournament I'll shoot with that hand—with one exception: when it's a choice of shooting with my right or using the mechanical bridge, I'll shoot right.

FORMAL LESSONS

I can't stress too much that if you're just starting out playing billiards, you should get formal instruction if you want to do well. If you start right, you'll play right.

With formal instruction, you'll not only learn proper technique but you should develop what we call "pool sense"—that intuitive knowhow, that judgment of which shots to take and which not to take, which shots can be made and which are impossible.

Any reasonably big city will have someone capable of teaching you. You can inquire at your local billiard parlor for the names of some top players and how to reach then. Call one of them up and get those lessons underway. It will probably cost you 20 or 25 dollars an hour, but it's an excellent investment if you're at all serious about playing.

Now, to be candid with you, just because someone is an excellent player is not positive assurance he'll be an excellent teacher. There are some fine players who can't teach at all. But they're not likely to take on a teaching assignment. And a person with a good knowledge of the game will usually be able to instruct you in the fundamentals and tell you what you're doing wrong. Knowing what's wrong is an important part of learning how to do it right.

PRACTICE

After you've taken basic instruction from a pro, the real learning begins. You've got to learn the fundamentals—stance,

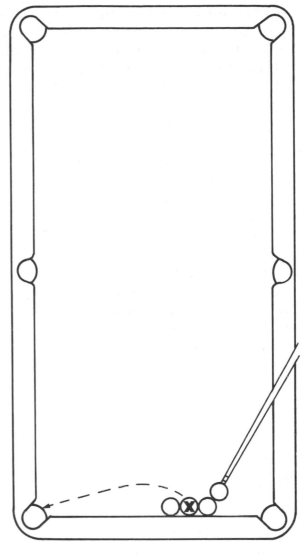

DIAGRAM 21.
Trick shot. If you *push* the cue ball above center with left-hand English, the center ball will be pocketed and the other two will not.

bridges, general pocketing of the ball —on your own. You do it through regular practice.

A good exercise is just to scatter the balls around the table at random and practice shooting. Put the balls all over the table and learn how to hit the cue ball in such a way that you drive the object ball into the pocket that you want. Learning to play position will come later from experience and from watching other, better players. First learn how to make the shots.

When I say practice regularly, I mean every day. You can't give it up for a month and then come back and expect to pick up at the level you left off. I used to practice four or five hours a day, but I think one hour a day is sufficient. If you overdo your practice sessions, you run the danger of working yourself into a state of boredom, which will defeat your purpose. Keep up the daily routine until you're good enough that it isn't necessary to practice as often. One word of caution: don't be like so many new players who get discouraged very easily. The game can't be learned overnight.

Practice With a Partner

Once you feel you're on the way to mastering the fundamentals, it's best to practice with somebody. There are several reasons for this: first of all, it will give you a sense of being in competition, and you'll try harder than if you're playing by yourself. Second, your opponent will be able to point out the mistakes that you make, mistakes you might not be aware of on your own. Don't be reluctant to take his or her criticism.

If possible, try to play with someone who's better than you are, because that's a player you can learn from. According to some opinions, a friend is the last one from whom you should seek advice. But my feeling is that if your friend can beat you, he or she probably knows more than you and can teach you something.

Play a Game

I recommend that when you have someone to practice with you play a regular game. For starters, I think you should play straight pool (see Chapter 3). The reason I feel this game is the best for beginners to practice with is that it gives experience with pocketing the ball, and it isn't as tough as some of the more complicated games.

Practice in one form or another is an unending necessity, even though the better you become, the less hours of practice you need. As you get better, you'll want to perfect particular shots. Eddie Robin, the ace three-cushion billiards player, says he spends hours practicing shots that he might never need in a match. But he wants to be sure that, if they do arise, he's seen them before and is capable of making them.

glossary

Angle: The relationship of the cue ball to the target or object ball; also, the relationship of the cue ball from its first to its second object. If you're trying for a simple carom, for instance, you would determine at what angle your cue ball must leave the first object ball to strike the second.

Angled: A situation in pocket billiards or snooker in which the corner of a pocket prevents you from shooting the cue in a straight line at an object ball.

Around the table: A situation in which you drive the cue ball to three or more cushions in an attempt to score, before or after hitting the first object ball.

Balance: The point on a cue stick at which the weight of the stick is even in both directions, toward the butt end and toward the tip.

Ball off the table: Usually, a jumped ball, one which, after a stroke, comes to rest elsewhere than on the bed of the table.

Ball on: A ball at which a player can shoot directly in a straight line. In snooker, a ball is on—that is, a player is said to "on a ball"—when that ball can be legally struck by the cue ball. Also, in pocket billiards, a ball may be "on a pocket" if it can be driven into a called pocket on a combination or kiss shot.

Bank shot: A shot that results when a player banks the cue ball or, in pocket billiards, drives an object ball against a cushion and then into a pocket from that cushion.

Bed: The playing area of the table.

Break: In all pocket games, the opening shot of the game, in which the player is required to "break" the object balls in a manner set forth by the rules of the game being played. In snooker, a break is a series of consecutive scoring strokes in one turn (inning) at the table.

Breeze: *See* Feather.

Bridge: The placement of the left hand (for right-handed players) on the table as it holds and guides the shaft of the cue in stroking. Also, a cuelike stick with a notched plate at the tip end, which a player may use as a bridge in shooting over a ball or in making a shot that cannot otherwise be reached.

Bust: Slang term for the opening of any game.

Butt: The lower, thicker portion of the cue stick, which is held by the player's power hand.

Call shot: In some games the player must call the ball he intends to make and the pocket he intends to drop it in. If he fails, it's a miss. Another name for the game of 14.1 continuous.

Called ball: In pocket billiards games, the ball a player announces he intends to score in a called pocket.

Called pocket: The pocket into which a player announces he intends to drop a called ball.

Carom: A carom in billiards is a score or a count, the result of the cue ball bounding from one object ball to another. A carom may be made by the cue ball glancing off one object ball directly into the second (or third) object, or by the cue ball glancing off the first object ball into a cushion and then into the second (or third) object.

Center spot: A spot in the exact center of the table on which a cue ball or an object ball may be spotted in games requiring the use of that spot.

Combination shot: A shot in which the cue ball strikes a ball that in turn hits the object ball and drives it into the pocket.

Count: A score. A point or a number of points, depending on the game. In most games of pocket billiards, for example, a count or score is one point. In rotation pocket billiards, a count is a score in which the scoring players get points corresponding to the number of the ball.

Cripple: A ball that can be easily pocketed.

Crutch: The mechanical bridge.

Cue ball: The white, unnumbered ball in pocket billiards and other games, which is struck by the cue stick and in turn strikes an object ball.

Cue ball in hand: A situation in which, as the result of a foul or error on the part of his opponent, or some other factor, the player puts the ball in play anywhere he chooses within the head string.

Cue stick: The instrument with which a player strikes a cue ball in pocket billiards and other games played on a pool table.

Cue tip: The leather end of the cue stick, which makes contact with the cue ball.

Cushion: The cloth-covered, resilient ridge that borders the inside of the rails on carom and pocket billiard tables. Usually made of rubber.

Cut: To strike a ball at an angle.

"D": An area marked on the table for snooker games.

Dead ball: A combination shot that can't miss.

Diamonds: Decorations around the rim of a billiards table, often used as guides for carom shots.

Draw: A stroking technique that allows the player to draw the cue ball back from an object ball. A *draw shot* is one in which the players apply draw to the stroked cue ball by hitting the cue ball below center.

English: A spin applied to the cue ball to control its action either before or after it hits an object ball by hitting the cue ball to the right or left of center.

Fancy shot: Usually an exhibition shot; a shot that requires unusual skill; a trick shot.

Feather: To hit a ball very thin.

Follow: A stroking technique that allows the player to make the cue ball "follow" in the same general direction as the object ball after it strikes an object ball. The opposite of *draw*. A *follow shot* is one in which the player has applied follow to the cue ball by hitting the cue ball above center.

Follow-through: Movement of the cue stick after it made contact with the cue ball, through the area that was occupied by the cue ball before it was struck by the cue.

Foot spot: A spot near the foot of the table, at the point where imaginary lines drawn from the center diamonds on the short rails and from the second diamonds on the long rails (near foot of table) intersect. The spot for the placement of object balls at the start of most billiard games.

Foot string: An imaginary straight line drawn through foot spot from one side of the table to another, across its width.

Foot of table: The short rail of a billiard table not marked with the manufacturer's nameplate, as opposed to the *head* of the table, which is marked by the manufacturer's nameplate.

Foul: Any infraction of the rules governing billiards. Fouls are usually penalized by the loss of points, the penalty depending upon specific game rules.

Foul stroke: An infraction of the rules in which the foul takes place as a result of the player's stroke. Pushing the cue ball is a foul stroke in most games. Double contact of the cue tip on the cue ball (two separate contacts) is a foul stroke.

Frame: *See* Inning.

Frozen: A term used to describe balls that are touching each other on the table. When object balls are frozen they remain in play as they are. When the cue ball is frozen to an object ball, player proceeds according to the rules of the game being played. A ball may also be frozen to a cushion—in other words, resting against a cushion.

Full ball: A situation in which a cue ball strikes an object ball exactly in the center. As opposed to half-ball, one-third ball, one-quarter ball, etc.

Furl: The decorative ring around the shaft of a cue stick, immediately below the cue tip.

Gather shot: A technique that allows a player to bring the object balls back into position for consecutive scoring.

Head of table: The short rail marked by the manufacturer's nameplate.

Head spot: A spot on the table near the head at the point where imaginary lines drawn from the center diamonds on the short rails and the second diamonds (near the head of the table) on the side rails intersect.

Head string: An imaginary line that, from the second diamonds on the side rails (near the head of the table), runs through the head spot. The area between the head string and the head of the table is referred to as *within the head string* or as a *balk*.

High run: The most consecutive balls a player has pocketed without a miss.

Hold: Usually, reverse English. The application of English to a cue ball, which tends to hold the cue ball back from the course the ball normally would take, having been driven in a certain direction.

Hugging the rail: A situation in which a ball, usually because of *hold English*, tends to stay close to a rail. Application of English may cause the ball to roll along the rail or cause it to bounce against the same rail one or more times as it travels along that rail.

Hustling: Method used by pool sharks to entice less skilled players into games for money.

Inning: A turn at the table. The duration of a player's stay at the table from the time he legally makes the first shot of a turn until he ends his turn, either by missing, fouling, scoring the maximum number of balls allowed, or terminating the game.

Jaw: Corner of a carom table or opening of pocket on pocket table.

Key shot: The next to last shot in straight pool, before the balls are reracked.

Kiss: A kiss is a carom. The cue ball may kiss from one object ball to another. An object ball, already struck by the cue ball, may kiss the second object ball either into or from the path of the cue ball. In pocket games, the cue ball may kiss from one object ball into another to score the latter ball.

Lagging: A method of determining which player breaks the balls to start play.

Each player takes a turn hitting a ball so that it bounces off the foot rail. The player whose ball comes back nearest to the head rail has his choice of whether or not to break.

Ladies' aid: A somewhat disparaging term for the mechanical bridge.

Line-up: A pocket billiards game. Also, the method of spotting the balls in a game of line-up.

Long: A term used when a ball comes off a cushion at a wide angle.

Long string: An imaginary line running from the foot spot to the center of the foot rail, on which balls are spotted in pocket billiards games when the foot spot is occupied or when more than one object ball must be spotted. The long string line is also extended beyond the foot spot for the placement of spotted balls, if the line between the foot spot and the foot of the table is totally occupied.

Mechanical bridge: The cuelike stick with a notched plate at the tip end, which a player may use as a bridge in shooting over a ball or in making a shot he cannot otherwise reach.

Miscue: A faulty stroke; faulty contact of the tip of the cue against the cue ball. A stroke in which the cue tip slips from the cue ball, not applying action as planned due either to a defective tip, improper chalking of cue tip, or, in many instances, to excessive English.

Miss: Failure by a player to accomplish what he intended on a stroke. A miss may or may not be a foul, depending on the rules of the game being played.

Natural: A simple shot; one which can be made directly (in pocket billiards) or as the result of a simple angle in carom billiards; a shot with a natural angle, as opposed to a shot that is "not on."

Nominated ball: In pocket billiards, a nominated ball is one that a player calls as the ball he intends to drop in a designated pocket. In snooker, a player "nominates" the ball he "is on" before making a stroke, unless his shot is obvious, or unless his opponent requests a nomination; or, he may nominate the "ball on" for his own protection, in the event of a subsequent protest by the opposing player.

Object ball: In pocket billiards and related games, the ball the player wants to pocket, or hit with the cue ball.

Pool: Another name for pocket billiards.

Push shot: Shoving or pushing the cue ball with the tip of the cue. Also, the contact of the cue tip on cue ball. Push shots are legal in pocket games if the stroke is made with what appears to be continuous, uninterrupted motion of the cue. The referee is the sole judge as to whether a player was guilty of an illegal push shot in pockets.

Pyramid: The placement of the object balls in pocket games when the balls are racked in a triangle at the foot spot to start a game.

Rack: The wooden or plastic triangle used to pyramid balls at the foot spot for the opening shot in pocket billiard games. Also, the grouping of the balls at the foot spot in pyramid formation after the triangle has been removed. For example, the player drives the cue ball into the rack on the opening shot.

Rails: The flat surfaces of the table, above the table bed from which the cushions slope. There are two end rails and two side rails. The rail marked with the manufacturer's nameplate is the head rail. The unmarked short rail is the foot rail. The rail to the right, when one is standing at the head and facing the foot, is the right rail. The other long rail is the left rail.

Reverse: English applied to put "hold" on the ball.

Rotation: The name of a pocket game in which the player must drive the cue ball against object balls in numerical order. Also, the sequence of play when two or more players are involved, as in "rotation of play."

Run: A series of consecutive scores or counts in one inning.

Safety: A defense measure to which a player can resort when confronted with a difficult shot. He sacrifices an opportunity to score as well as his turn at the table in an attempt to leave a difficult shot for his opponent.

Scratch: Generally, an unanticipated development as the result of a player's stroke, which may or may not be a foul, depending upon the situation and rules of the game. A player may scratch the cue ball into a pocket; he may "scratch" a point as the result of a kiss, which point he would not have otherwise, etc. Usually, it involves the end of the inning, and in certain games a loss of a point as well. There are times when a player will scratch intentionally rather than give his opponent a set-up.

Set-up: An easy shot.

Shaft: The thin, upper part of the cue stick, where the tip is located. The shaft is supported by the bridge hand or mechanical bridge in taking a shot.

Shark: An adept pool player. Sometimes an unscrupulous player who hustles unsuspecting prey into games for money.

Slate: The basic undermaterial of a pool table bed.

Snooker: A game played on a special sized table with special balls and cue sticks. Red unnumbered balls and six numbered balls must be pocketed alternately, then numbered balls made in rotation. A popular game in Great Britain.

Snookered: To be unable to shoot the cue ball in a direct line at the object ball, which is on, is to be "snookered."

Spot Ball: A ball placed on the foot, head, or center spot at the start of a game, or after having been illegally pocketed or forced off the table, or which is spotted as the result of a specific game requirement, as when the 15th ball interferes with racking in 14.1 continuous pocket billiards.

Spot shot: A shot in which the player shoots at a ball that has been placed on a spot.

Spotting: The replacement of balls on the table as required by rules of the game.

Stick it: To hit the cue ball in such a way that it stops in its tracks after it makes contact with an object ball.

Stop shot: A shot in which the cue ball stops on contact with an object ball. *See* Stick it.

Straight pool: Pocket billiards.

Thin: A term applied to a cue ball that barely touches the side of an object ball.

Triangle: Triangular wooden or plastic frame used to rack up balls in pyramid fashion at beginning of pocket billiards games, and in 14.1 continuous billiards when there is only one ball left on the table.

Value of balls: The scoring value of balls depends on the rules of particular games. In rotation pocket billiards, for example, each ball is worth points equivalent to its own number.

index